SINGLE *to* GOD

100 Personal Prayers
by Single Adults

DOUG FAGERSTROM
general editor

kregel
PUBLICATIONS

Grand Rapids, MI 49501

Single to God: 100 Personal Prayers by Single Adults

Published by Kregel Publications, a division of Kregel, Inc., P.O. Box 2607, Grand Rapids, MI 49501. Kregel Publications provides trusted, biblical publications for Christian growth and service. Your comments and suggestions are valued. For more information about Kregel Publications, visit our web site: www.kregel.com.

ISBN 0-8254-2585-9

Printed in the United States of America

1 2 3 4 5 / 05 04 03 02 01

Contents

When we have a severe trial to undergo, or some danger or some suffering to face, go aside to pray.

—Charles de Foucauld

Very early the next morning, while it was still dark, Jesus got up, left the house and went to a solitary place, where he prayed.

—Mark 1:35

This book is dedicated to single adults who need to find a special, quiet place with God where they can pray.

For some, this book will be
an emergency room,
or a waiting room,
or major surgery,
or critical care,
or a gentle release and rest
from life's mountains and valleys,
or a celebration of God's blessings.

The prayers in this book were written by single adults from all over the USA.

They were slightly edited, mainly for length.

These prayers have brought the writers through tough days and glorious days.

These prayers can bring you through the same.

Foreword

"O what peace we often forfeit, o what needless pain we bear, all because we do not carry *everything* to God in prayer." The timeless words of the hymn still explain the stress in the lives of many adults. It's not that we do not believe in prayer—we do, especially in the crisis moments of our lives. Rather, stress is common because we do not pray. We do not pray across the landscapes of our souls, and many things in our hearts and on our minds go unexpressed in prayer.

"Why should I read someone else's prayers?" Good question. Throughout the history of the church, prayers have been recorded, memorized, passed down to the next generation. Consider the rich prayers of the psalmist, which have encouraged Christians through the ages. Reading someone else's prayers can be beneficial for several reasons.

You can be *strengthened*. There will come those moments when you cannot pray or don't know how to pray. This book offers a chance to "eavesdrop" on prayers written by single adults who have faced the same issues and the same crises you face.

You can be *encouraged*. Sometimes it is a phrase, a sentence, a thought in another's prayer—whether written or spoken—that resonates within your heart, too.

You can be *reminded*. Sometimes you have so much on your mind that you fail to remember someone or something that needs prayer. In reading *Single to God* you may be surprised and may find yourself saying, "I've never thought of praying about that." These prayers will, time and again, remind you of the tender graciousness of a God who cares deeply about you and is eager to hear your prayers.

It's been a long time since I prayed "Now I lay me down to

sleep. . . ." Sometimes I needed my mother's prompting in composing my earliest prayers. These prayers will help you and me. They can be a starting point for a deeper relationship with God.

Scripture reminds us that "we ought always to pray." It's the believer's privilege.

—HAROLD IVAN SMITH

Preface

True, whole prayer is nothing but love.

—St. Augustine

Pray as you can, not as you can't.

—Dom Chapman

In the same way that a child cannot draw a bad picture so a child of God cannot offer a bad prayer.

—Richard Foster

The intimate language of love with God is prayer. Sometimes the words are few. Sometimes the prayer is long, endless. Prayer is always an essential part of our lives in Christ, vital to our relationship with him.

Many times we just don't feel like praying. Other times the words are not available to meet the feelings or circumstances recently experienced. Often we struggle in our disbelief, and wonder if God is listening or even cares.

The truth is that God does care, all the time, and he never stops listening. The comfort is that no prayer is a bad prayer. We must pray every time we have a need.

This book is dedicated to singles who desire to pray but struggle to find the right words and confidence to pray. The Scripture reference at the top of each page is a reminder of God's grace, mercy, love, and promises. The written prayer has already been prayed by another and is yours to share. The quotation at the end is an everyday reminder that God hears and answers.

Don't just read this book. Use it. Make it a daily companion and friend. Pass this new friend to a friend, thereby introducing your heavenly friend.

PART 1

Prayers *of* Adoration, Praise, *and* Thanksgiving

1

A Prayer *of* Adoration *for* God's Love

For God so loved the world that he gave his one and only Son, that whoever believes in him shall not perish but have eternal life.

—John 3:16

Dear Father in heaven, I thank you for your love. It awes me to think that, although you have only one Son, you were willing to allow him to die a terrible death so that my sins and the sins of my family and friends could be forgiven. He was innocent, and I praise and thank you that you allowed your Son to take all the blame for us.

Thank you, Father, that all who believe in their hearts and confess with their mouths that they have sinned will be forgiven and will become your children. Thank you for your free gift of love.

I praise you, Jesus, and thank you for paying the price for me. With gratitude I thank and praise you for your unfailing and everlasting love. Amen.

Betty

Love is the verb of which God is the object.

—L. M. Starkey Jr.

2

A Prayer *of* Adoration *for* God's Goodness

Give thanks to the LORD, for he is good; his love endures forever.

—1 Chronicles 16:34

O LORD, our Lord, how majestic is your name in all the earth!" [Ps. 8:1]. All creation shouts your praise. "What is man that you are mindful of him?" [Ps. 8:4]. Thank you, Lord, for your incomparable, unchanging goodness. You display your goodness to us in endless extravagance. You lavish us with the richest of gifts.

It is hard for me to comprehend that you would create the birds and the sky and the sea and the grass and trees and every living creature for the enjoyment of people. That seems extravagant. I feel unworthy. But you did all this for me.

You provide everything that I need—the rain, the snow, the sunshine, and the thunder—and plenty that I think I need. You are generous with friendships, laughter, tears, passion, and more.

Yet, if there were nothing on this earth for us humans to enjoy, if I were to awaken from my sleep to find that all of these good things had been a dream, your goodness would still radiate in the hearts of men and women, and I would still be compelled to cry out to you in praise and adoration. It is enough that you chose me to be your child, Lord, that you grant me the privilege of coming boldly before your throne.

I love you, Lord, for who you are and for your goodness. Amen.

Char

God is so good, God is so good, God is so good, he's so good to me.

—African Christian folk song

A Prayer *of* Adoration *for* God's Mercy

Because of the LORD'*s great love we are not consumed,*
for his compassions never fail. They are new every morn-
ing; great is your faithfulness.

—Lamentations 3:22-23

Lord, I'm on top of the world.
  I am glad and thankful
  for all the things that have come my way.
  I worship and adore you.
Thanks for your mercy and grace.
  Without it I would not be.
  Your greatness is above all things.
  Your love is lavish.
What can I give you that is not yours now?
  Is there anything that I have not yielded?
I offer myself as a gift to you,
  even though I am afraid.
  I know you are gentle and kind.
I see my inadequacies and fallacies clearly.
  Thanks for your forbearance and patience.
Now, at this juncture, I thank you
  for the options that are available,
  for the freedom to choose,
  for the yeses and nos that guide me.
Thanks for friends and elders who care.
Amen.

Glenn

Kind hearts are here; yet would the tenderest one
have limits to its mercy; God has none.

—A. A. Proctor

A Prayer *of* Adoration *for* God's Majesty

Then I heard every creature in heaven and on earth and under the earth and on the sea, and all that is in them, singing: "To him who sits on the throne and to the Lamb be praise and honor and glory and power, for ever and ever!"

—Revelation 5:13

Father God, we marvel at your awesome majesty. You are the almighty God, the Creator of all things, and by you all things hold together. You are the eternal, loving Father, clothed in light, righteous, and all-powerful. You are our God, and we are the sheep of your pasture.

We honor you as the only one worthy of having first place in our lives. You are light and truth, and in you there is no darkness at all. You have extended your loving-kindness to us and have become our peace.

How great and mighty are your ways, O Lord. They are beyond our finding out. We honor you and bow down before your throne.

You, God, are worthy of our highest praise and worship. Amen.

Dianne

Depend upon it, God's work done in God's way will never lack God's supplies.

—J. Hudson Taylor

A Prayer *of* Adoration *for* God's Holiness

Exalt the LORD our God and worship at his holy mountain, for the LORD our God is holy.

—Psalm 99:9

Dear Lord, you are an awesome God! Thank you, Father, for being a perfect and holy Father and for sending your Son, Jesus. I am thankful for your perfection, holiness, and great blessings to me. You make me feel completely protected; for your perfect wisdom I can trust you. I can lift up my problems and worries to you, and you still love me. You know me so well you overwhelm me in your understanding of my needs.

Every day I think about how blessed I am that you provided me with a way to learn, with a way to eternal life, and with earthly things such as great Christian friends and fellowship and the ability to earn a living. Without your divine knowledge how could you provide me with all that I need?

Dearest Father, I adore you, I praise you, I love you, I trust you, and I look forward to the day I can bow to you in your great kingdom. You are a most holy God and infinite. For that, dear Lord, I, a finite person, am forever grateful. Amen.

Trudy

The essence of true holiness consists in conformity to the nature and will of God.

—Samuel Lucas

A Prayer *of* Praise *for* Hope *and* Peace

Peace I leave with you; my peace I give you. I do not give to you as the world gives. Do not let your hearts be troubled and do not be afraid.

—John 14:27

Most precious heavenly Father, I praise you for bringing me safely down the pathway of life this far. Yes, even before I truly understood how much you loved me and had a special plan for me, you were leading and caring for me. In countless ways you have shown me that you exist—in the beauty that surrounds me, through Christian friends, and in answered prayers. I have seen your work in my life and in the lives of others.

No, you have not sheltered me from pain and sorrow, but during those times you have given me daily strength and the knowledge that you are near. You help me get through every hardship in my life. Everything is possible with you, and there is nothing I cannot do as long as I lean on you and ask for your help.

Help me to be content with my life in serving you in whatever capacity I am able, wherever you lead. I thank you, Father, for your love, comfort, peace of mind, and daily strength. I pray that others will see Jesus in me, that they will know I am yours and you are mine by the way I live my life.

In the precious name of Jesus, Amen.

Anne

Life with Christ is an endless hope, without him a hopeless end.

—Anonymous

A Prayer *of* Praise *for* Victory *in* Christ

But thanks be to God! He gives us the victory through our Lord Jesus Christ.

—1 Corinthians 15:57

Jesus, how comforting to know that
through all my trials and convictions you were
    there to establish justice;
through all my afflictions you were there to heal;
during my times of loneliness you were there to
    bring solace;
when I experienced doubts and anxieties, you
    were there to bring reassurance;
as I tried to piece my life back together, you
    were there to make me whole;
when I felt like giving up, you were there,
    encouraging me to try once more;
as weariness overwhelmed me, you were there
    to support me;
when my dreams were shattered, you were there
    with visions of hope.

How wonderful to know that with you by my side I was able to overcome any obstacles and be victorious. And all you wanted was for me to ask.

Venus

Let us keep to Christ, and cling to him, and hang on him, so that no power can remove us.

—Martin Luther

A Prayer *of* Praise *for* Assurance *of* God's Salvation

And this is the testimony: God has given us eternal life, and this life is in his Son. He who has the Son has life; he who does not have the Son of God does not have life.

—1 John 5:11-12

Dear Father in heaven, you are a glorious and wonderful God, a God of all wisdom and power. I know that I am a sinner.

Lord, I want to give you all the glory and honor for sending your Son, Jesus Christ, into this world to die for my sins. Thank you for the grace you have given me, even when I didn't deserve it. I praise you because I know that I cannot earn my salvation. My salvation rests on faith in your Son, Jesus Christ. Thank you for opening my eyes and for giving me a personal relationship with you.

I thank you that because of your Spirit my life has changed. I have a new life on earth and in eternity with you. Lord, thank you for formations of my personal relationship that the Holy Spirit gives me. Thank you for your Word, Christian friends, the power of prayer.

I pray this only through the power of my resurrected Lord and Savior, Jesus Christ. You alone deserve all the praise and glory. Amen.

Scott

To be like Christ is to be a Christian.

—William Penn

A Prayer *of* Thanksgiving *for* God's Many Gifts

Praise be to the God and Father of our Lord Jesus Christ, who has blessed us in the heavenly realms with every spiritual blessing in Christ.

—Ephesians 1:3

God, thank you for my rest last night, for this day, and for this time you've given me to spend with you. I went outside this morning, and the air was crisp and fresh from the rain. The sunrise was in full force; what a great way to start the day!

I thank you for the wonderful family that you have given me. Through all of our trials and struggles over the years you have kept us together and our love strong.

Lord, I thank you for the church and the singles group you've brought me. Through this group's love and support you have reached down and tapped resources that I didn't think I had. You have given me the courage to drop my masks and be the person you created. The people in the group have taught me much about you and about myself.

Thank you for the very special friends you have given me. I now have more friends than I've ever had; they are friends who really care about me, and I really care about them. I thank you that you've allowed us to be candid with each other without the fear of rejection.

I thank you that you've helped me tear down the walls of life and fear, letting you come in to show me your grace, acceptance, and forgiveness. Amen.

Leigh

God's gifts put man's best dreams to shame.
—Elizabeth Barrett Browning

A Prayer *of* Thanksgiving *for* Friendships

A friend loves at all times, and a brother is born for adversity.

—Proverbs 17:17

As iron sharpens iron, so one man sharpens another.
—Proverbs 27:17

Father, my heart is overwhelmed with your gift of friendship. As I get to know you more and understand your unconditional love, I am humbled by it. Thank you for friends who love me unconditionally. Thank you for the model that we have in you to build friendships.

Thank you for the friends in my life who challenge me and encourage me to develop a deeper relationship with you. Father, at times if it were not for friends and their influence on my life, I would never know the precious friendship and relationship I have with you.

Thank you for the family of friends that you have blessed me with. I am a better person because of them. Second to your incredible gift of salvation, your gift of friendship is right at the top.

Help me this day, Father, to be a friend to someone else, to love at all times. Help me to encourage a friend to grow in your love just as my friends have done for me.

In your precious name, Amen.

Donna

Do good to thy friend to keep him, to thy enemy to gain him.

—Benjamin Franklin

PART 2

Prayers When I Struggle Most

11

A Prayer When No One Seems *to* Care

Cast all your anxiety on him because he cares for you.
—1 Peter 5:7

Father, you are my best friend. When no one else seems to care, you are close to me. I can come to you, before your very throne, and you hear me. You know the pain of loneliness. You know my every need and the desires of my heart.

I trust you to care for me, to love me, and to see me through anything that may come my way. Father, help me to forget myself and be more like Jesus Christ. Encourage me to pour out my love to those who are hurting and lonely. When I love others unselfishly as your Son Jesus loves, I will know the love, peace, and joy that only he can provide to me and my friends.

Father, I love you. Amen.

Jane

Of all the things which wisdom provides to make life entirely happy, much the greatest is the possession of friendship.

—Epicurus

A Prayer When I Feel That God Has Let Me Down

Remember your leaders, who spoke the word of God to you. Consider the outcome of their way of life and imitate their faith.

—Hebrews 13:7

O Lord, I don't understand. I thought I was in your will. I thought the wants I had were your wants for my life. Now I'm confused and I doubt. I don't know what to do or where to go. I feel lost and hurt.

Lord, help me to see through your eyes, from your perspective. Help me to see the value of this time in my life. I know you are working for my good. Let me see how these days fit into your plan for my life.

Lord, please help me to heal and then help me to go on. I know that you are looking out for my life, loving me, carrying me, and cheering me on all at the same time. I love you for that, but I need you now more than ever. Lord, please help me to see what you see.

I ask this as if Jesus were asking it for me. Amen.

Julie

Before us is a future all unknown, a path untrod; beside us a friend well loved and known—that friend is God.

A Prayer When I Have Been Let Down *by* My Friends

Do not reject me or forsake me, O God my Savior. Though my father and mother forsake me, the LORD will receive me.

—Psalm 27:9-10

Dear heavenly Father, I have a great pain very deep in my heart. I feel very lonely right now because a friend I used to spend a lot of time with has a boyfriend, and I never see her or hear from her.

Lord, I am very hurt because I feel used and rejected by this friend. We used to visit every weekend and spend quality time together.

The thing that hurts me most is that her departure from my life was so abrupt. I now wonder if our previous relationship really meant much to her.

Dear Father, I pray that you will give me a peace about this relationship, and that you will supply me with the strength to forgive. Help me to see the situation through your eyes and to be more sensitive to my friend's current needs and not only to my own.

I know that I am never alone. You are always with me to help me carry the burdens of my life, and I thank you, Father, for your wisdom and guidance in this situation.

I pray these things in the name of Jesus. Amen.

Jennifer

Actions, not words, are the true characteristic mark of the attachment of friends.

—George Washington

A Prayer When I Feel
Ready *to* Give Up

But those who hope in the LORD *will renew their strength.*
They will soar on wings like eagles; they will run and
not grow weary, they will walk and not be faint.

—Isaiah 40:31

Dear Lord,
Hold me tonight, Lord.
Wrap your arms around me.
Hold me tightly, Lord.
Don't ever let me go.
    Keep up the fight, Lord, the one to set me free.
    Show me your might, Lord; make me pure as gold.
Let me feel the pain.
Don't let me be restrained.
Give me the heart that I desire.
And lead me in your ways.
    Test me with fire
    Before I get too old.
    Let my ways be your ways;
    Let my days be your days.
I'm crying to you, Lord, with love.

Kevin

The world beginning to get you down? Feeling rotten? Too tired to pray? Let me suggest one four-letter word that God loves to hear us say to him: Help!

—Charles Swindoll

A Prayer When I Find
I'm Under *a* Lot *of* Pressure

Then maidens will dance and be glad, young men and old as well. I will turn their mourning into gladness; I will give them comfort and joy instead of sorrow.

—Jeremiah 31:13

Father, at times I feel as if I'm hanging on to a loose branch or worse yet, being swept by a perpetual roaring wave. I am constantly struggling to make ends meet, consistently slaying dragons to protect my family, continuously battling peer pressure and wanting to remain virtuous.

O heavenly Father, please calm the raging waters of my existence. Mend my broken heart. Extract all bitterness and unforgiveness from my soul. Breathe strength back into my weary arms. Guide me to make the right decisions for this family. Light the path to freedom from all this pressure, and fill my life with peace and love. Amen.

Venus

Humanity is never so beautiful as when praying for forgiveness, or else forgiving another.

—Jean Paul Richter

A Prayer When Injustice Prevails Against Me

Blessed are you when people insult you, persecute you and falsely say all kinds of evil against you because of me. Rejoice and be glad, because great is your reward in heaven. . . . But I tell you: Love your enemies and pray for those who persecute you.

—Matthew 5:11-12, 44

God, as I walk around this cold, dark house with no one to reach out to, I wonder where you are. Why can't I feel your arms around me? Wasn't the cancer enough? Wasn't the mutilation of my body enough? Did my husband leaving me for a woman half his age have to be in the plan? You never give us more than we can stand? Well, right now I feel like I'm teetering on the edge of the cliff, and it's a long way to the bottom.

I read all the promises in the Bible, and most of the time I feel your peace. But when I roll over in bed, wanting to be comforted after a bad dream, the bed is empty. Please, God, heal my broken heart and help me forgive this man who left me when I needed him most.

God, give me strength to live each day the very best way I can. Take away the bitterness I feel when I'm at the cancer clinic and see other husbands comforting their sick wives. God, take away the nightmares, the anger, and dry my tears with your promises. Give me patience while I wait to discover your plan for my life. Thank you, God, for being near me.

Betty

We can always count on Jesus to be there for us.

A Prayer When I Am
Attacked *by the* Enemy

*Be self-controlled and alert. Your enemy the devil prowls
around like a roaring lion looking for someone to de-
vour. Resist him, standing firm in the faith.*
—1 Peter 5:8-9

Lord, I thank you for this present circumstance I am in. This is not
to say that it is what I prefer. My thanks comes from the confidence
I have in you, your Word, and its promises.

Lord, it comforts me to know that when the saints of the Bible
focused on you, you listened and acted on their behalf. I praise you
that you are the same yesterday, today, and forever. You said, "Do
not be afraid or discouraged because of this vast army. For the battle
is not yours, but God's" [2 Chron. 20:15]. Thank you that I need not
fight this battle alone. Give me strength to stand and see your salvation at work. I will not fear or be dismayed. Tomorrow I will face
the enemy and be victorious, for you are with me.

In preparation for the battle, I put on the full armor. I wear the
breastplate of righteousness, your righteousness, O Lord. I gird my
loins with truth, your Word. I put the sandals of peace on my feet—
the peace your gospel has brought me. I place the helmet of salvation on my head. I hold the sword of the Spirit, which is the Word of
God, in my hand. And I cover myself from head to foot with the
shield of faith, faith in you, Lord Jesus. Faith is the victory. Into your
hand I commit my all. Amen.

Mike

All my theology is reduced to this narrow compass—
Jesus Christ came into the world to save sinners.
—Archibald Alexander

A Prayer When I Am Attacked *by* My Own Flesh

What a wretched man I am! Who will rescue me from this body of death? Thanks be to God—through Jesus Christ our Lord!

—Romans 7:24-25

Heavenly Father, thank you for loving me and for always being ready to listen. Thank you for the blessings I've received already and for those I know you have in store for me. But Lord, I'm fighting with myself again!

Father, I need your help. You have given me this human form, and you know the problems that come with it. I need your help to bring control to my humanity.

Please help me to remember that my human reactions, responses, and desires must always be considered first, before any action is taken. Help me keep my tongue in check, my body pure, my ego down, and my hope and faith ever growing. I know what I want to do, but I don't always succeed that way. You know I fall, and I pray that I will always get up and turn to your guidance once again.

Be with me now, and help me be all that you would have me to be. Help me always remember who I am and what I stand for.

In Jesus' name, Amen.

Brenda

The dying Jesus is the evidence of God's anger toward sin; but the living Jesus is the proof of God's love and forgiveness.

—Lorenz Eifert

A Prayer When I Face Temptation

No temptation has seized you except what is common to man. And God is faithful; he will not let you be tempted beyond what you can bear. But when you are tempted, he will also provide a way out so that you can stand up under it.

—1 Corinthians 10:13

O God, my God! I want to do something that you don't want me to do. O Lord, open my spirit and mind and remind me of how much you love me. Help me to look realistically at the consequences of choosing evil. Help me to envision the blessings when I choose what is right.

My heavenly Father, remind me of how you gave your Son. Remind me of how much your Son suffered so that I can have life and hope.

O God, show me the way that you have provided for me to escape this temptation. Deliver me from evil. Thank you for hearing the anguish and turmoil of my heart. Thank you for delivering me.

I rest on your strength. Amen.

Dave

The only safe spot on earth where the sinner can stand—Calvary.

—D. L. Moody

A Prayer When I Have Sinned

If we confess our sins, he is faithful and just and will forgive us our sins and purify us from all unrighteousness.
—1 John 1:9

Dear Lord, here are my sins. I want to give them to you. You see, they have kept me from reading your Word and talking to you until now. And I have tried to pretend that you are not around.

Please take these sins, as you promised, and wash them away with your precious blood. Then give me the faith to carry on with you alone.

Lord, I thank you for the tears that I cry, even though I am a man and our culture says that men don't cry, and for reminding me through these tears that I am not just a man. Thank you for reminding me that I am your son and that your Holy Spirit is in my life. Thanks for helping me to cry over my sins, just as you cried over my sins.

Please give me a fresh start today and forgive me of my sins. Let me feel the love that I know you have for me. I no longer want the pain from the daily routine of "push and shove."

Refresh my heart. Fill me with your Spirit;
This vessel in which I dwell—I need you to steer it.

With all my love and pain, I pray as your son. Amen.

Kevin

I believe that one of the greatest therapies God ever gave to man was the therapy of forgiveness. Without it we would live in a constant state of guilt that could never be removed.

—Jim Smoke

PART 3

Prayers During Times *of* Great Need

A Prayer When I Need Love

For I am convinced that neither death nor life, neither angels nor demons, neither the present nor the future, nor any powers, neither height nor depth, nor anything else in all creation, will be able to separate us from the love of God that is in Christ Jesus our Lord.

—Romans 8:38-39

Lord, thank you for your Word that is true and that stands forever. Thank you for your love expressed to me in your Word.

Today I feel I don't matter to anyone. In fact, I feel I don't matter to you. I have made mistakes and have not performed to the expectations of myself or others. I feel used and unappreciated.

But thank you for your love that never fails, that has been with me from the beginning and will be with me to the end. Thank you for your love that is unconditional and not based on my performance. While I was the worst sinner, you loved me enough to send your Son to die for me.

Forgive me for believing the lies from myself, the world, and Satan that say I don't matter when you tell me that I do.

I receive your unconditional love today. Fill me full of this love. Help me to remember that I am lovable because you love me and for no other reason.

Thank you for hearing my prayer. Amen.

Kathy

Love has power to give in a moment what toil can scarcely reach in an age.

—Johann Wolfgang von Goethe

A Prayer When I Need Strength

*It is God who arms me with strength and makes my way
perfect.*

—Psalm 18:32

God, help! I'm hurting. Thank you for your steadfastness. In a society that changes quickly and is so fast paced I cling to the constant that you are in my life.

Lord, once again I need the encouragement and peace that I can get only from you. I need motivation and the strength to get through another day. I'm afraid of the uncertainties that I have to deal with today. I'm tired of hurting. I need a break in the storm.

Help me to remember past times that were difficult, when my pain was overwhelming, and how you have healed me both physically and emotionally.

Thank you for bringing me through difficult times. Thank you in advance for giving me strength for today. Amen.

Amy

> The Great Physician now is near,
> The sympathizing Jesus;
> He speaks the drooping heart to cheer.
> Oh, hear the voice of Jesus.
> —William Hunter

A Prayer When I Need
to Be Encouraged

*For everything that was written in the past was written
to teach us, so that through endurance and the encouragement of the Scriptures we might have hope. May the
God who gives endurance and encouragement give you
a spirit of unity among yourselves as you follow Christ
Jesus.*

—Romans 15:4-5

Lord, I need you right now. I never believed my heart could hurt
this bad. It constantly aches from actions and words that say, "I
don't love you. Go away." Why don't they accept my love for them?
What is it that turns them away? My love just doesn't seem to be
good enough. I don't understand why I'm being rejected. I didn't do
anything to deserve it.

Lord, I need to know you still love me. Your Word says you do,
but I struggle to believe it because of the hurt I feel now. I do believe
your promises and I know you care. Lord, hold on to me through
this time and show me your way for my life. Carry me through this
hardship.

Thank you for never letting go of me or turning me away. I will
trust in you. I love you, Lord! Give me a heart to love others again, to
love them the way you love me.

Rick

Under the shadow of earthly disappointment, all
unconscious to ourselves, our Divine Redeemer is
walking by our side.

—E. H. Chapin

A Prayer When I Need Grace

Let us then approach the throne of grace with confidence,
so that we may receive mercy and find grace to help us
in our time of need.

—Hebrews 4:16

Dear Jesus, I've been taking inventory of my life, and you seem to be far away. Years ago I prayed the sinner's prayer. I confessed you as Lord and Savior then, but of late I haven't prayed or worshiped. I have been quick to become angry and slow to listen. I have not loved my neighbor; in fact, I've treated him sometimes as my enemy. I certainly have not prayed for him. I have been pretty cavalier about my life and about your death and resurrection.

Lord, I know that I have mistreated my sisters in Christ. Lord, I know that I have not been faithful with my money. Lord, I know that I have crushed others with my comments rather than build them up. Jesus, I confess my sins. I repent. Fill me with your Spirit.

Praise be to God. He is slow to anger and full of compassion. He chooses to forgive and forget. He clothes me with clothes that are white, representing my new cleanness in Christ. He encourages me to lower my shield and to confess my sins to others.

Once more I am at peace with God. God has been at peace with me since the day I claimed his Son's blood on my behalf. Today we can live together in the reality that I am a prince of the kingdom of Christ.

Bill

Marvelous grace of our loving Lord, Grace that exceeds our sin and our guilt!

—Julia H. Johnson

A Prayer When I Need Mercy

You are forgiving and good, O Lord, abounding in love to all who call to you. Hear my prayer, O LORD; listen to my cry for mercy. In the day of my trouble I will call to you, for you will answer me.

—Psalm 86:5-7

Lord,
I love you and fear you.
All that I am I give to you:
   my strength, will,
    my health, mind, heart, and talents.
I have been using them, overusing them, and maybe
   abusing them.
Forgive me.
I have been losing my heart.
   It has grown hard.
May it open up and grow new life.
May I receive grace and mercy as I obey the Word
   that challenges
    my will.
May my will be never so impassioned or stubborn
   that it cannot heed the wisdom and restraint
    of the Almighty and his servants.
Forgive my ambition.
May I slow down and enjoy life.
May I grow in faith.
I fear to ask you. But to ask it is a good thing,
For you are good.
Amen.

Glenn

Mercy is when God withholds what we do deserve.

A Prayer When I Need Assurance

Then Jesus declared, "I am the bread of life. He who comes to me will never go hungry, and he who believes in me will never be thirsty."

—John 6:35

Heavenly Father, there are times when I wonder if you hear me crying, because I feel I haven't the strength to struggle through another day of heartache, another night of tears. Where are you? And how can you possibly hear my prayers when there are thousands of others asking for your help at the same time I am?

Your Word tells me that you will never allow me to thirst or to be hungry, that you are with me always. I know that all I need to do is ask in Jesus' name, with a trusting heart, and you will provide for my needs.

You must laugh at how easily I seem to forget all of the times you have answered my prayers; forgive me for so easily forgetting. I cannot begin to number the times you have provided food, financial help, strength, contentment, peace of mind, laughter, faithful Christian friends, and encouragement.

Help me trust you more. Help me, Father, to never forget how much you love me, how much you provide for me.

In Jesus' name, I pray. Amen.

Anne

Prayer is not conquering God's reluctance but taking hold of God's willingness.

—Phillips Brooks

27

A Prayer When I Need Wisdom

If any of you lacks wisdom, he should ask God, who gives generously to all without finding fault, and it will be given to him.

—James 1:5

Lord, I don't know what to do! This situation has me totally confused. I wish I could look into the future. It surely would make my handling of this situation a lot easier. But then, you do know the future. You see everything from beginning to end.

Not only that, you understand me perfectly—the way I think and feel. You know what I prefer and all the reasons why I prefer it. Lord, it's beyond me to know the next step to take, but certainly you are able to show me. Guide me and lead me in the way that best honors you. I will follow you in whatever direction you lead.

Thank you, Lord, for hearing this prayer. I'm waiting on you for the answer. Amen.

Rick

The greatest good is wisdom.

—St. Augustine

A Prayer When I Need Direction

Trust in the LORD *with all your heart and lean not on your own understanding; in all your ways acknowledge him, and he will make your paths straight.*

—Proverbs 3:5-6

O Lord, my heavenly Father, please help me remember that you love me as much as you love Jesus. May I live and breathe the fact that you want to prosper me and not harm me. You want to give me a hope and a future.

With this confidence, I trust you to guide me. I put my small, weak hand in your loving, kind, and powerful hand. You will lead me one step at a time.

Thank you, Lord Jesus. Amen.

Dave

I have been driven many times to my knees by the overwhelming conviction that I had nowhere else to go.

—Abraham Lincoln

A Prayer When I Need Patience

*James, a servant of God and of the Lord Jesus Christ, To
the twelve tribes scattered among the nations: Greetings.
Consider it pure joy, my brothers, whenever you face
trials of many kinds, because you know that the testing
of your faith develops perseverance.*

—James 1:1-3

Dear Lord, I come to you today with a heavy heart. I pray to you to give me more patience with my mother. Please help me to control my temper with her and not snap at her every time she asks me something. I need help in trying to get along with her from day to day. I pray that you will soften my heart for her and teach me to love her. Please use the Holy Spirit through someone else to reach her, because I feel that I cannot. I know everything does not happen overnight.

I also pray for patience at work. Please help me to learn my job the right way and not be in a hurry all the time so I won't make as many mistakes.

In my social life, I pray that you will help me slow down. Teach me to wait and to remember that good things really do come to those who wait.

In Jesus' name I pray. Amen.

Michelle

The most useful virtue is patience.

—John Dewey

A Prayer When I Need *a* Friend

My command is this: Love each other as I have loved
you. Greater love has no one than this, that he lay down
his life for his friends.

—John 15:12-13

Dear Lord, everything that I have comes from your hand. You have given me all that I need and much, much more. But something is missing in my life.

Lord, to me a flower is an example of that once-in-a-lifetime love that makes a person's life complete. Lord, flowers are beautiful, especially when the sun shines on them and they move gracefully in the wind, as if they are dancing to their favorite song in harmony with one another. Oh, to have someone pick me from among many flowers is my dream.

Lord, many nights I lie awake and cry until I have no more tears. I miss gentle touches and caresses and a man's arm around me, holding me tightly and making me feel secure. I haven't experienced that for over five years.

Yes, I love you. Your love is more than enough for me, but at times it's hard to face my singleness. Please, Lord, consider me adequate to make someone else's life more complete.

I pray this as your loving child. Amen.

Dawn

Of all earthly music, that which reaches farthest into
heaven is the beating of a truly loving heart.

—Henry Ward Beecher

PART 4

Prayers When My Emotions Are Out *of* Control

A Prayer When I Feel Discouraged

Have I not commanded you? Be strong and courageous.
Do not be terrified; do not be discouraged, for the LORD
your God will be with you wherever you go.

—Joshua 1:9

Dear Father in heaven, I'm tired. Sometimes I feel like Elijah right after the big showdown on Mount Carmel [1 Kings 19], full of discouragement and not wanting to face this world another day. Each day has too many battles—tensions at work; relationships that drain my energy; commitments; and responsibilities to friends, family, and church. I give of myself to others all day long, and most of the time it seems to make no difference.

Lord, I don't want to be full of self-pity. That is a favorite trap of Satan's. I come to you for encouragement. This old world tears me down, but you alone build me up. Remind me again of two things—your power and your love—and then I can go on. I never can escape your presence and loving hand.

So feed me, Lord, with the bread of your Word and let me drink from the well of living water that never runs dry. Only then will I have the strength to face the disappointments of this life and set my heart on things above.

Thank you for your promises. Amen.

Lynda

Happiness is neither within us nor without us; it is the union of ourselves with God.

—Pascal

A Prayer When I Feel Rejection

I waited patiently for the LORD; *he turned to me and heard my cry. He lifted me out of the slimy pit, out of the mud and mire; he set my feet on a rock and gave me a firm place to stand. He put a new song in my mouth, a hymn of praise to our God. Many will see and fear and put their trust in the* LORD.

—Psalm 40:1-3

Dear Father in heaven, Why? It's not fair, Lord. I feel I have been tossed aside like an old, worn-out shoe. I feel I no longer belong to anyone or that anyone needs me. The choices have been made about my future, and I did not have a say. I feel like a victim. Sometimes the pain is so great the only thing I can say is, "Help me, Lord."

Thank you for loving me even in my most unlovable moments. Even though you have promised never to leave me or forsake me, I have to admit that because of the rejection my faith is sometimes weak.

Help me, dear Lord, to trust again. I don't want to face the future alone. Please go with me and hold my hand. Show me that your love is different from the human love we experience in this life.

Fill me with your love and kindness so I in turn can reach out to others who have been rejected. Help me to make a difference by turning my pain into something good.

Thank you for your acceptance of me. Amen.

Sharon

No man loveth God except the man who has first learned that God loves him.

—Alexander Maclaren

A Prayer When I Feel Miserable

In my distress I called to the LORD; I cried to my God for help. From his temple he heard my voice; my cry came before him, into his ears. . . . He reached down from on high and took hold of me; he drew me out of deep waters.
—Psalm 18:6, 16

God of love and mercy, when I was far from you and cried out to you, you heard me. In your compassion you reached down and lifted me from the low point of my life. You delivered me from the hands of my enemy and those who would harm me—even from myself.

How loving and tenderhearted you are, O God, to those who call out to you in the name of your precious Son, Jesus; your mercies and compassion toward me are more than I can comprehend. Daily you care for my unspoken needs, even before I can think of them or ask you. You rain your abundant mercies and grace on me.

Though I am a pauper by worldly standards, I am rich because I have you—a holy and righteous God, my defender, protector, and provider. You are to be lifted up and praised above all else; only you, O God, are worthy of my praise and adoration. May your wonderful name be echoed in the hills as my lips bring forth your name.

Praise your name, O Lord. Praise your holy name. Amen.

Jeannie

To be content with little is difficult: to be content with much—impossible.
—Marie von Ebner-Eschenbach

A Prayer When I Feel Great Pain

He will wipe every tear from their eyes. There will be no more death or mourning or crying or pain, for the old order of things has passed away.

—Revelation 21:4

Dear God, it's another day. The nausea still lingers, just as on most days. My muscles are weak, but the headache is gone. God, my life is limited now. I can't hold a job, I can't clean my own house, I can't do my yard work. Society says I'm "unproductive."

Please, God, tell me that just being here, being alive is okay. Please, God, don't let Satan tell me I'm worthless. Make my limited life have meaning.

I can still love and care about my girls, my family, my friends. I can still talk and laugh and listen and offer advice from having lived forty-three years. God, forgive me when I am weak and tempted by the values of society. Give me your strength, hope, and peace.

God, teach me to be content with just being. Amen.

Betty

I am always content with what happens; for I know that what God chooses is better than what I choose.

—Epictetus

35

A Prayer When I Feel Confused

God is our refuge and strength, an ever-present help in trouble. Therefore we will not fear, though the earth give way and the mountains fall into the heart of the sea, though its waters roar and foam and the mountains quake with their surging.

—Psalm 46:1–3

Dear God, you are my anchor, but sometimes I am hopelessly confused. No matter what direction I take, I go nowhere. Lord, I don't understand. I search your Word and pour out my heart, but I seem to have made no progress. And when I do make progress in a certain direction, convinced it is your leading, it is suddenly taken away. Therefore, I'm sometimes afraid to step forward for fear of having to retrace my steps.

Father, once again I surrender to you the right to change my plans. I will follow you, even when it hurts. Please direct me. Show me that you are using me even in my present circumstances. Please calm the confusion in my heart.

Like a ship tossed back and forth by the wind,
I am battered back and forth,
Twenty feet one way, thirty feet the opposite.
Lord, are you not my anchor?
Why is the rope so long?
Shorten the rope, God, or calm the storm!

Lynda

Never be afraid of giving up your best, and God will give you His better.

—Hinton

A Prayer When I Feel Lonely

I am with you always, to the very end of the age.
—Matthew 28:20

Dear Lord, as I talked to you out of my loneliness, feeling worthless and unloved, I visualized myself in a clearing in the mountains. It was early evening, cold, gray, and windy. I called out, "Jesus, Jesus, it's me, Rhoda."

In my heart you answered, "Yes, Rhoda, I've been waiting for you." You asked me to come with you.

We followed a path to a cottage. A gentle trickle of smoke came from the chimney, and the windows had a welcoming glow of warmth and life. On entering, I at once had a feeling of comfort and ease. I could smell the aroma of fresh bread baking and coffee brewing. Some people were laughing together by the fireplace.

You, Jesus, sat down at a big wooden table in the kitchen and I sat down with you. I poured out my heart to you. After a while I realized it was getting dark outside and that I would have to leave. I could not stay in that wonderful refuge. I had to go back out and face my grim circumstances.

A great sadness came over me, but I stood up and prepared to return to my cold dark world. I got my coat, opened the door, and turned to say good-bye, and there you were putting on your coat to go back into my world with me.

Lord, thank you for reminding me that you go with me even through the bleakest times. Thank you for the gift of your friendship, faithfulness, and love. Amen.

Rhoda

He who has no friend has God.
—Egyptian proverb

A Prayer When I Feel Afraid

*So do not fear, for I am with you; do not be dismayed,
for I am your God. I will strengthen you and help you; I
will uphold you with my righteous right hand.*

—Isaiah 41:10

*Be strong and courageous. Do not be afraid . . . for the
LORD your God goes with you.*

—Deuteronomy 31:6

Lord, sometimes I feel afraid, because I'm all alone now, and I don't
know what's going to happen to me tomorrow.

In Isaiah 41:10 you tell me not to be fearful, for you are with me.

I know that by your grace I am your child. Help me to remember
that I am not alone, that you are with me every minute of the day
and night. Help me to trust that nothing will happen to me today
that you don't already know about.

I pray for the strength and wisdom I need for today. Thank you
for your love. Thank you, Lord, for your promises, and thank you for
your Holy Spirit who comforts me even when I am afraid.

I cling to your righteous right hand. Amen.

Betty

Courage is resistance to fear, mastery of fear—not
absence of fear.

—Mark Twain

A Prayer When I Feel Exhausted

He gives strength to the weary and increases the power of the weak.

—Isaiah 40:29

Come to me, all you who are weary and burdened, and I will give you rest. Take my yoke upon you and learn from me, for I am gentle and humble in heart, and you will find rest for your souls.

—Matthew 11:28–29

Lord, when I entered this race, I had visions of easily conquering all of the turns and hills of the course. I thought I would glide each step of the way.

Well, right now I'm tired. I didn't expect the hills to be this big, and I didn't plan for these detours.

I have a long way to go. I know why I'm running this race, but I'm losing sight of the finish line. Please protect my mind; help me to remember the reasons why I'm here.

Jesus, I want you to be my teammate, to run alongside me, to set a pace that will challenge me but that will let me finish strong. And if you have to carry me somewhere along the way, that's okay. What matters is that I finish.

And for the next race, Lord, I want you to be my coach. Help me to train and prepare well, and please don't let me start without you. The hills are too big and the curves are too wide for me to run by myself. Amen.

Bill

Worship renews the spirit as sleep renews the body.
—Richard Clarke Cabot

A Prayer When I Feel
No Hope *for* the Future

"For I know the plans I have for you," declares the LORD,
*"plans to prosper you and not to harm you, plans to give
you hope and a future."*
—Jeremiah 29:11

Praise the comforter, the counselor of peace.
Glory to God! Amen.
O my mighty, wonderful God:
　Your Word is righteous.
　Your grace is sublime.
　Your mercies are tender.
But, oh, how you cut into my heart!
I am sightless.
I am weak in spirit.
I am . . .
　But you are God.
　You are the righteous one.
　You are the only hope,
　　My deliverer,
　　My daily bread,
　　My warmth from your light.
I am wounded, then healed.
I am made weak to be strengthened.
I am saved to be a witness.
Amen to the almighty being!
Amen to the holy presence!
Amen to the great I AM!

Glenn

Man thinks, God directs.
　　　　　　　　—Alcuin

A Prayer When I Feel
That My Dreams Are Broken

*The righteous cry out, and the L*ORD *hears them; he delivers them from all their troubles. The L*ORD *is close to the brokenhearted and saves those who are bruised in spirit.*

—Psalm 34:17–18

Precious heavenly Father, I love you, and I thank you for your Son, who is my best friend, and that he loves me and never leaves me.

Father, as you know, many painful things have happened these last few weeks. I have lost much. It is as though everything has been ripped away from me. There has been criticism, which seems to be never ending, and tears have been shed. My heart has been broken and my spirit crushed. What about my hopes and dreams? In a split second they were shattered. I have been made to feel worthless and a failure. Why go on?

But no matter what other people do or say to me, I now know that in your eyes I am not and never could be worthless. I am your child. The one thing they cannot take away is you and your love. Through all of the pain, I have made a decision to trust you, knowing that you only want what is best for me.

Thank you, Father, that you never leave me. Thank you for the wonderful people you have brought into my life—people who love and care for me just as I am, even when I don't love myself.

In the name of Jesus, Amen.

Deb

No one is useless in this world who lightens the burden of it to anyone else.

—Charles Dickens

PART 5

Prayers When I Need God's Help

A Prayer *for* God's Help
During Those "Ugly" Days

This is the day the LORD has made; let us rejoice and be glad in it. O LORD, save us; O LORD, grant us success. Blessed is he who comes in the name of the LORD. From the house of the LORD we bless you.

—Psalm 118:24–26

Thank you, Lord, for making me the unique person I am. Help me to know I am beautiful inside and outside, even though I may not feel pretty or handsome and may have bad feelings stored up inside. Help me to know you love me regardless of what I look like or what I do or what I say. Help me to be appreciative of the talents you have blessed me with. I know you don't make junk, Lord, and I take comfort in that thought.

Help me to know I can count on you for strength in hard times and good times, for I know you always listen, Lord. Please give me patience in waiting on you and the strength to carry on, day by day. Help me to show others that they are truly loved by you, regardless of what they say or do. I pray that I would see the error of my ways and seek your guidance in all that I do. Please let the opportunity arise today for me to tell someone else she is a beautiful and wonderful child of God. Amen.

Susan

Beware of despairing about yourself: you are commanded to put your trust in God, and not in yourself.

—St. Augustine

A Prayer *for* God's Help During Stressful Times

Therefore we do not lose heart. Though outwardly we are wasting away, yet inwardly we are being renewed day by day. For our light and momentary troubles are achieving for us an eternal glory that far outweighs them all.
—2 Corinthians 4:16-17

Dear God, everyone has stress in their lives. It's the modern way to live. Demands are everywhere. Even the demands I put on myself are getting harder to meet. During these times, God, I try my best to be in control, to handle stress my way.

When will I learn? Why do I put all the pressure on myself when you are waiting for me to ask for your help? When I ask for your help, you are ready to respond. No, the stressful situation does not vanish because I ask. What vanishes is the anxiety, and it is replaced with a confident feeling that, with your help, I can make it through another day. Thank you. Amen.

Jan

Let my soul calm itself, O Christ, in thee.
—Harriet Beecher Stowe

A Prayer *for* God's Help During Uncertain Times

But as for me, I will always have hope; I will praise you more and more.

—Psalm 71:14

Father in heaven, I thank you that in these uncertain times I have a good job. I thank you that almost everyone at my place of work is a practicing Christian and I can talk to them about my walk with you. I pray for wisdom and strength to be a faithful witness for you.

Thank you, also, that all of my material needs are met. I am grateful I do not make so much money that I could have everything I want. I thank you for the appreciation you have given me of my material goods, and I pray that I will never take them for granted and stop thanking you for them.

Lord, let me never brush aside the incredible act of your grace and love; keep it ever at the front of my mind. Through Christ you have given me love and hope. Thank you for your gift in the Holy Spirit, my inner strength. Lord, I pray that each day I might lean more on the Holy Spirit to guide me and less on my own strength. Only then can I receive the gift of a continually growing relationship with you.

As I came home from work today, the sun was slowly setting in the west. Lord, what a beautiful end to this wonderful day! Help me always to remember to look around me and notice the glorious gifts you give us all every day.

More and more often I want to say "thanks." Amen.

Leigh

Optimism is the faith that leads to achievement. Nothing can be done without hope.

—Helen Keller

A Prayer *for* God's Help During Job Difficulties

You then, my son, be strong in the grace that is in Christ Jesus. . . . Endure hardship with us like a good soldier of Christ Jesus.

—2 Timothy 2:1, 3

Dear Father in heaven, I thank you for the many prayers you have answered in my life recently. You have given me a precious son, a new home, a new sitter for my son, a new school for my son, and a new job. But Lord, why this job? I know I am the lowest on the totem pole, but why do I have to work with these older people who are so stubborn and set in their ways? They gossip and spread rumors. Nothing I do seems good enough.

I am frustrated and I don't know what to do. I let them get me angry and upset, and I'm almost in tears half the time. I am even starting to bring the stress home with me, and it's not fair to my son.

Lord, please show me how to deal with these people. Help me to show them your love by being patient and kind and by controlling my temper. Help me to be open to their suggestions and learn from their experience. Please take away this stress and help me learn to relax. Please guide my every step and every word that comes from my mouth. Please show me why you have put me in this job, and help me to bring my coworkers to know you.

In Jesus' name, Amen.

Tonia

Great works are performed not by strength but by perseverance.

—Samuel Johnson

A Prayer *for* God's Help During Physical Pain

He heals the brokenhearted and binds up their wounds.
He determines the number of the stars and calls them
each by name. Great is our Lord and mighty in power;
his understanding has no limit.

—Psalm 147:3-5

Dear God in heaven, tomorrow is another day for a chemotherapy treatment. How can I do this again and again? I need your strength because I just don't have it on my own. Only you, God, know how I really feel inside. My body is weak; my spirit is defeated. Why me, God?

I remember being able to walk and run and climb with no pain. Now I dream of running through a beautiful green field. God, you know that I awaken from those dreams with tears running down my face. I hate being trapped in this sick body; only with your help can I accept it and do my best with it.

Right now, God, I need all the strength you can give me to get through tomorrow. I hope I can do it with a smile and a kind word for someone else who has been given this same cross to bear. Hold me in your loving arms, God, and make me as strong as I need to be. Don't let me be a coward. Make me what you want me to be, and place me where you want me to go.

God, don't let all of this pain be for nothing. Amen.

Betty

In the highest class of God's school of suffering we learn not resignation nor patience, but rejoicing in tribulation.

—J. H. Vincent

A Prayer *for* God's Help During Times *of* Loss

Call upon me in the day of trouble; I will deliver you, and you will honor me.

—Psalm 50:15

Dear Lord, because of Mother's suicide I have made some interesting discoveries about suffering. Most people don't want to deal with it. I can mention that this has happened, and people immediately change the subject without even uttering an "Oh, how horrible!" or "I'm really sorry!" Then I think of those who are in wheelchairs or seriously burned, and how we look away from them. If we ignore the suffering, we think it won't affect us.

Then I think of you, Jesus, and how you sought out those who suffered and walked among them, taking their suffering on yourself. You know how much I miss my mother. I cannot understand why you allowed this to happen. I know that you are listening, carefully listening, and embracing my spirit with your sorrow over my being disciplined by this pain. You point to the cross and then to the tomb. Soon the hope of resurrection from my sorrow begins to take hold, because you, unlike the people who turn away, have experienced my sorrow with me.

"I can bring life out of death" is your promise of the empty tomb. I rest on that. Amen.

Mary

God washes the eyes by tears until they can behold the invisible land where tears shall come no more.
—Henry Ward Beecher

A Prayer *for* God's Help During Failure

In this you greatly rejoice, though now for a little while you may have had to suffer grief in all kinds of trials. These have come so that your faith—of greater worth than gold, which perishes even though refined by fire—may be proved genuine and may result in praise, glory and honor when Jesus Christ is revealed.

—1 Peter 1:6-7

Lord, I feel like such a failure. I feel humiliated, angry, and hurt. Have I really done a terrible wrong? I keep going over and over it in my mind. What happened? Why? What will people think? How could I have failed so miserably? Or do I only feel like a failure? I feel awful now and I don't know what will happen next.

Father, help me look at this with your eyes. I'm embarrassed. Is that just my pride? I want to please you most of all, but pride in my accomplishments does not please you, especially if it does not acknowledge your help. I'm ashamed that I failed. Is my shame because I try to live up to a standard which is not yours? Please help me sort out these things. Where I have sinned, forgive me, and use this experience to teach me to be more like Jesus. Help me to honestly do my best and to hold your values as mine. Father, I trust you. My security is in you—not in how well I perform. Help me not to forget that.

You are my hope for the future, Lord. Amen.

Pat

He who stands upon his own strength will never stand.

—Thomas Brooks

A Prayer *for* God's Help During *a* Crisis

We were under great pressure, far beyond our ability to endure, so that we despaired even of life. Indeed, in our hearts we felt the sentence of death. But this happened that we might not rely on ourselves but on God, who raises the dead. . . . On him we have set our hope that he will continue to deliver us, as you help us by your prayers.
—2 Corinthians 1:8-11

Dear heavenly Father,
My strength is weak.
I have gotten myself into earthly problems, and
   the burden is heavy;
I can no longer find the strength to fight my
   way out.
I have tried various substances to hide from
   this crisis.
I cannot hide any longer, Lord.
I cannot carry these burdens by myself.
I am down on my knees asking for your help. I
   have no strength left.
I am praying for your strength to carry me
   through this heavy-burden crisis.
I ask for help in your Son Jesus' name.
Amen.

Jim

Faith is the act of trust by which one being, a sinner, commits himself to another being, a Saviour.
—Horace Bushnell

A Prayer *for* God's Help
During *a* Transition

I will lead the blind by ways they have not known, along unfamiliar paths I will guide them; I will turn the darkness into light before them and make the rough places smooth. These are the things I will do; I will not forsake them.

—Isaiah 42:16

Dear Father, I thank you for your continuing faithfulness in all the circumstances of my life. When things around me seem out of control, I know that nothing is out of your control. I confess that I resist change, and this transition is taking me into the unknown. Please help me to yield to you any uncertainty or anxiety that these circumstances may bring. Help me to take your hand and walk by faith with you into this unknown time.

My desire is to trust you one step at a time with simple, childlike faith, believing that you will bring me victoriously through to the other side. I pray that you will use this period in my life to teach me and mold me more fully into the person you desire me to be. May you use this transition to more completely fulfill your purposes for my life.

I thank you in advance for all that you are going to do. Amen.

Dianne

The only important decision we have to make is to live with God; he will make all the rest.

A Prayer *for* God's Help During Family Problems

Do not let any unwholesome talk come out of your mouths, but only what is helpful for building others up according to their needs, that it may benefit those who listen.

—Ephesians 4:29

Lord, family life has been complicated by stressful circumstances. The pressures we face seem to be altering not only our family members' expectations of each other but also what each of us is capable of handling. Consequently, feelings have been hurt and past pains have surfaced. Frustration, bitterness, helplessness, tension, and an unforgiving spirit are robbing us of some of the joys that we should be sharing with each other. They are eroding our hearts and lives.

Lord, I know that I have no right to complain—problems in many other families are far worse—but these are big ones for my family, and without your strength and loving arms around us we cannot get through this. Please give us the endurance and the courage to face the things that we fear most. Calm our anxious hearts. Help us forgive each other and ourselves so that we can be free to love and build each other up.

Be our God of peace. Amen.

Kirsten

God has not called us to see through each other, but to see each other through.

—Horace Moody

PART 6

Prayers *for* Those Things I Cannot Control

Lord, I Cannot Pray Right Now

In the same way, the Spirit helps us in our weakness. We do not know what we ought to pray for, but the Spirit himself intercedes for us with groans that words cannot express. And he who searches our hearts knows the mind of the Spirit, because the Spirit intercedes for the saints in accordance with God's will.

—Romans 8:26–27

O Lord, I don't even know what to say to you right now. I'm completely confused. Lord, please listen to your Holy Spirit inside of me and what he asks of you on my behalf. Lord, all I can ask is that your will be done.

I ask this as if Jesus were asking it for me. Amen.

Julie

The fewer words the better prayer.

—Martin Luther

Prayer requires more of the heart than of the tongue.

—Adam Clarke

Lord, I Am Not Motivated *to* Do *the* Right Things

Finally, brothers, whatever is true, whatever is noble, whatever is right, whatever is pure, whatever is lovely, whatever is admirable—if anything is excellent or praiseworthy—think about such things. Whatever you have learned or received or heard from me, or seen in me—put it into practice. And the God of peace will be with you.
—Philippians 4:8-9

Dear God, I was brought up to know the difference between right and wrong. I also know what a conscience is. When things happen not to my liking, why do I want to take the easy way, which is usually the wrong way?

God, you never promised me that living a Christian life would be easy, but you did promise to be my strength and guide. I am asking you today to help me choose the right way, no matter how tough it seems.

Thank you, God. Amen.

Jan

Obedience must be the struggle and desire of our life.
—Phillips Brooks

Lord, I Am Having Nightmares

You have filled my heart with greater joy. . . . I will lie down and sleep in peace, for you alone, O LORD, make me dwell in safety.

—Psalm 4:7-8

Dear Father in heaven, I pray when I lie down to sleep, as the psalm says, that you will let me sleep in peace, for you alone, Lord, make me dwell in safety.

But Lord, take out of my mind all these thoughts that are racing through it, all my worries of everything that has happened and that will happen. Help me to realize that I do not need to worry about my life. Help me to believe that what happens in my life, what I eat or wear, or any other of my concerns that keep me awake all night almost every night are in your hands. Give me peace in the fact that as you take care of the birds and flowers you also surely take care of me.

Please clear my mind of all the worries and problems that keep me awake at night. And when I do get to sleep and have nightmares, refocus my mind on that which is good. I need an inner peace, to trust you in all things, and to get a good night's sleep tonight.

God, you are my refuge. Amen.

Jim

Where there is peace, God is.

—George Herbert

Lord, *the* Anger Is Destroying Me *and* Others

In your anger do not sin; when you are on your beds, search your hearts and be silent. Offer right sacrifices and trust in the LORD.

—Psalm 4:4-5

Gracious heavenly Father, I ask for guidance in the area of anger. My response of getting angry, Lord, does not solve problems. I am aware of how selfishness is in control when I am angry. The anger takes hold of my thoughts toward others.

People I come in contact with during the time I am angry do not get ministered to; just the opposite happens. They do not receive any gentleness or kindness, and certainly no joy, peace, longsuffering, or love.

Dear Lord, when I hang on to anger, it turns into rage, making me even more mean spirited toward other people. Also, I often have an attitude of bitterness toward life. Bitterness spawns resentment and hate in my mind, emotions, and will.

I must confess the anger as sin; I agree with the Bible that anger is a sin. I also am aware of how I miss the mark when I feel anger toward another person.

I pray to you, Lord, to take the need to be angry away from me. I also ask you, in the name of Jesus, my Savior, to replace it in my heart with a healing gentleness.

I trust in you and thank you in Jesus' name for what you will in my life. Amen.

Roy

I could not live in peace if I put the shadow of a willful sin between myself and God.

—George Eliot

Lord, I Need You
to Heal My Past

With it he touched my mouth and said, "See, this has touched your lips; your guilt is taken away and your sin atoned for."

—Isaiah 6:7

I, even I, am he who blots out your transgressions, for my own sake, and remembers your sins no more.

—Isaiah 43:25

Dear Father in heaven, greet me with a sign of your love. My past always seems to lurk beyond the conscious part of my mind. Frequently it crowds up to the surface, disturbs me, and interferes with my life. It intrudes into my relationships with you and others. It causes me not to do things that need to be done.

Father, the worst result of my reactions to past hurts is that they keep me separated from you. When I was a child the defensive reactions may have been okay, but now that I am an adult they are sometimes wrong and sinful. The patterns block communication and fellowship with you. Forgive me of this sin.

Please remind me over and over again how deep and vast is your love, which overcomes all the past hurts. Thank you that your love gives me strength to get through the struggles. In the end, I know I will be more like precious Jesus and will bring glory to your name. Amen.

Richard

God be thanked for that good and perfect gift, the gift unspeakable: his life, his love, his very self in Christ Jesus.

—Maltbie D. Babcock

Lord, *the* Guilt Hurts Deeply

Rescue me from the mire, do not let me sink; deliver me
from those who hate me, from the deep waters.

—Psalm 69:14

Dear Father in heaven, hear my prayer. Please listen as I call out to you. At times the sadness and loneliness push on my chest like a stone, and I cannot find the answers to the hopelessness in my heart. Please guide me away from the suffering that causes my spirit to fall and the guilt in my heart that causes me to turn and run from you.

I do know that through your love you have given me a gift, a very special gift: the ability to make choices. But I am guilty of making unwise choices. Yet you have shown me that even if I lack faith in myself, you have faith in me, and in your unwavering love I can find inner peace.

Heal my heart with your love and show me that each of us has a reason for living. Bless me with your grace, forgive my sins, and teach me that only by you, through you, and with you beside me can I be at peace. Let me rejoice in my being one of your unique and unrepeatable miracles. Amen.

Craig

Repentance is the heart's sorrow, and a clear life ensuing.

—William Shakespeare

Lord, *the* Shame Doesn't Seem *to* Go Away

Let us draw near to God with a sincere heart in full assurance of faith, having our hearts sprinkled to cleanse us from a guilty conscience and having our bodies washed with pure water. Let us hold unswervingly to the hope we profess, for he who promised is faithful.

—Hebrews 10:22-23

Father, thank you for your forgiveness of my sin. Thank you for Jesus and his precious blood that he shed for me and my salvation. I know and I believe that I am forgiven, and you have forgotten my sin. But Father, I have not forgiven myself, and I cannot forget.

The guilt and shame will not go away. It makes me sick. How do I forgive myself? Father, please relieve me of these memories and heal me.

I give the shame and guilt to you and ask you to remove them from me. Help me daily to let go and leave them with you. Help me to hold fast the hope that is my salvation in Christ.

I claim your promise to forget my sin and cast it as far away as the east is from the west. I ask that you will create in me a clean heart, that I may know you and serve you and not sin against you. Amen.

Jane

A bad conscience embitters the sweetest comforts; a good one sweetens the bitterest crosses.

—Wendell Phillips

Lord, I Need Your Strength *in a* Tough Decision

But show me unfailing kindness like that of the LORD as long as I live, so that I may not be killed.

—1 Samuel 20:14

Dear heavenly Father, I thank you for the opportunity to pray to you. Lord, a man worked for me for several years. You know who this person is. He is a very devious and simple-minded person. He has caused my family, my friends, my business, and me a lot of grief.

I prayed for help, and you removed him from our lives.

Lord, he has come back, asking if he can return to the business to work. I pray for the strength and wisdom to say no to this troubled young man. But should I say yes? I don't know.

I know you will give me the wisdom and courage as I have asked you, and I thank you for the answer to come.

I pray these things in your Son Jesus' name. Amen.

James

Learn to say no; it will be of more use to you than to be able to read Latin.

—Charles Haddon Spurgeon

Lord, I Need Your Help
to Slow Down *and* Listen

*Search me, O God, and know my heart; test me and
know my anxious thoughts. See if there is any offensive
way in me, and lead me in the way everlasting.*
                                                —Psalm 139:23-24

Father, it's been a good evening at the edge of Lake Michigan. As I
sat and listened to the waves hitting the shore I read your Word.
Tonight I read a few verses on listening. Wow! I was once again
reminded of how I don't really spend as much time listening to you
as I do talking to you and being discouraged when I think you aren't
listening to me.

Forgive me, Lord. You always listen, but I need to stop talking
and complaining and listen to you more.

Thank you for giving me a valuable lesson on listening as I sat
here this evening in the beauty of your creation on the beach. Amen.

Deb

Oh, how great peace and quietness would he pos-
sess who should cut off all vain anxiety and place all
his confidence in God.
                                                —Thomas à Kempis

Lord, I Am Having *a* Tough Time Being Single

For he chose us in him before the creation of the world to be holy and blameless in his sight. In love he predestined us to be adopted as his sons through Jesus Christ, in accordance with his pleasure and will—to the praise of his glorious grace, which he has freely given us in the One he loves.

−Ephesians 1:4-6

Lord, I am having a tough time being single. You know it was my desire and dream to have a loving husband and children, to have a wonderful Christian family. I never thought this nightmare of divorce could happen.

Lord, you know my whole world has fallen apart. You are aware of all the pain, the hurts, the many frustrations, the awful bitterness and loneliness. Please heal my wounds. Help me pick up the broken pieces. Mold me and make me a better person. Use me for your service, honor, and glory. Teach me and help me now as I walk alone to be strong and to cast all my care on you.

I don't always see your plan, especially in my being single once again. Was this part of your plan? I know not what the future holds, but thank you, Lord, for holding my future. Show me the hope and plans you have for me. Thank you for putting single Christian friends into my life who give me support, love, and prayers. Help me to be of good courage; take away my fears. Amen.

Sandy

O Lord, that lends me life, lend me a heart replete with thankfulness.

−William Shakespeare

PART 7

Prayers When I Cannot Fix *or* Make Things Better

God, I Don't Know What *to* Do

Do not conform any longer to the pattern of this world,
but be transformed by the renewing of your mind. Then
you will be able to test and approve what God's will is—
his good, pleasing and perfect will.

—Romans 12:2

God, I don't know what to do about many different things. Many things I don't understand. I don't know why divorce had to be part of my life. Then, alone, I had to go through the removal of a tumor and the fear of cancer. We had promised to care for each other in sickness and in health. Thank you, God, for being with me in the cold operating room, warming me with your love. Thank you for not breaking your promise to never leave me.

I don't know what I would have done without you, God, when I heard that my dear father had had a severe heart attack. Help me to keep believing that you are still in control of all things and make no mistakes.

I don't know what to do about my children, Lord. I would love to shelter them from the mistakes and pain and hurt. I lift up all my children, my parents, and my life to you. Protect us from harm. Guide us in all our ways and always keep us close to you. Help me to move on in love and kindness.

Teach me your perfect will for my life. Amen.

Sandy

The tears of Christ are the pity of God. The gentleness of Jesus is the long-suffering of God. The tenderness of Jesus is the love of God.

—Alexander Maclaren

God, I Don't Think That I Can Go On

I will refresh the weary and satisfy the faint.
                                        —Jeremiah 31:25

God, I woke up this morning with the sun shining on my face. You have given me the gift of life for one more day. Help me, God, to see all the blessings you have given me. Help me see past the cancer to the beautiful things in my life.

I have two beautiful daughters who love me and, now that I am so sick, take care of me. I have wonderful friends who have seen me through the darkest of hours. You gave me a love for life and a deep sensitivity for other people.

Help me hang on to these things when the drugs bring me down to that hopeless feeling. Thank you, God, for all the extra days you've given me since my cancer was diagnosed. Thank you for the laughter that I have in my life. Please, God, don't let me lose my sense of humor!

And, God, when I'm tempted to ask, "Why me, Lord?" remind me, "Why not me, Lord?" Thank you for the good days. I know you have a plan for my life that contains good days and bad, but I'm not ready to go to my eternal home yet.

Please, God, give me many more days like this one. Amen.

Betty

Faith builds a bridge across the gulf of death.
                                        —Edward Young

God, I Am Losing My Grip

Therefore I will boast all the more gladly about my weaknesses, so that Christ's power may rest on me. . . . For when I am weak, then I am strong.

—2 Corinthians 12:9-10

Lord, I'm playing tug-of-war and desperately trying to hang on with all my might, only to find myself falling in the mud. Humiliated. Frustrated.

You created me. You know how easy it is at times for me to lose focus. Thank you for your constant care and love for me.

I know that I need to yield my will and desires completely to you. Thank you for your patience and understanding. I need the strength and tenacity to hold on. I need to remember my goals and regain my perspective. Help me to see not only my own narrow world and circumstances, but the big picture through your eyes.

Thank you that in my times of greatest frustration I can see your glory and your purpose in my life. Amen.

Amy

By his trials, God means to purify us . . . and bring us into implicit, humble trust in himself.

—Horace Bushnell

God, I Need *a* Reason *and* Purpose *to* Live

For to me, to live is Christ and to die is gain.
— Philippians 1:21

Father, my very soul aches with confusion and with pain. I have a sense of drowning in an anger that I willingly have given to you over and over. Yet it keeps sneaking back.

Will this foolishness I continue to perceive in myself ever go away? Can you help me to find a reason for living along with a sense of direction and belonging?

I need to be needed! Do you really need me, God? Will you use me for your purpose?

Right now I feel too hurt even to care. I want to run and not look back. But I did look. Surprisingly, through the hurt I could see the healing. I know, because I believe you. That's it, isn't it God? The only reason I go on is my belief in you.

I used to sing. The stress of the past three years has taken its toll on my voice. For me that constitutes a nightmare. God, for your glory, I will sing again; I will be back in the choir. Only you can make the sound come out again.

You are showing me, even now, the servant's heart. I am here. I will serve you. You were always available to me, and now I choose always to be available to you.

I will live for you, Christ. Amen.

Dolores

The King of love my Shepherd is,
Whose goodness faileth never;
I nothing lack if I am his
And he is mine forever.
— Sir Henry William Baker

God, I Need *to* Discover Who I Am

Yet to all who received him, to those who believed in his name, he gave the right to become children of God.
—John 1:12

Lord, I come to you disappointed, disillusioned, and unfulfilled again. It seems whenever I get my eyes off you and begin to concentrate on my circumstances or on what others have that I don't have, I lose sight of the dreams and ambitions that you have given me. You made me with special passions and longings to direct me toward completing my portion of your big plan. Forgive me, Lord, for getting sidetracked again.

God, I need to discover who I am again so that I can be used of you in that special role that you have for me to play. It isn't good enough to hear others tell me who I am or to search my innermost part to find the answer. I know where the answer lies. My identity is found in you. It matters not what others think; what matters is who I am in your eyes.

Lord, I trust you and I surrender myself to you. Please speak to me in this quiet moment and cause me to have inner peace and understanding. Give me direction and a true sense of my identity before you. Cause me to seek you with all my heart, for as I learn to know your mind I will have a better understanding of myself and of my role in your kingdom. Amen.

Char

All that I am I owe to Jesus Christ, revealed to me in his divine Book.
—David Livingston

God, My Relationships Are *a* Disaster

A new command I give you: Love one another. As I have loved you, so you must love one another. By this all men will know that you are my disciples, if you love one another.

—John 13:34-35

Father, I am thankful that your Word clearly indicates that you chose me as an object of your love and that it was not anything I did. I am also thankful that you know me better than I know myself, and you chose to love me in spite of what I am or am not. You also know what I need in my relationships. I don't have to tell you what a disaster they are.

Just when I think I am making progress, another disaster explodes in my face. O Lord Jesus, help me, I pray.

"In you, O LORD, I have taken refuge; let me never be put to shame; deliver me in your righteousness. Turn your ear to me, come quickly to my rescue; be my refuge, a strong fortress to save me. Since you are my rock and my fortress, for the sake of your name lead and guide me" [Ps. 31:1-3].

Lord, all I know is that you are the only one who knows I mean well. Help me, Lord, I pray, and thank you.

I praise your holy name. Amen.

Michael

God has given us the choice whether or not we follow him; but in reality, we are always at his mercy.

67

God, I Cannot Forgive That Person

*Be kind and compassionate to one another, forgiving
each other, just as in Christ God forgave you.*
                                —Ephesians 4:32

*If you forgive men when they sin against you, your heav-
enly Father will also forgive you. But if you do not forgive
men their sins, your Father will not forgive your sins.*
                                —Matthew 6:14-15

Lord, I have accepted your forgiveness in the past; but now I have
been wronged so much that I do not know how to, or maybe do not
want to, forgive. Please give me a desire to forgive. I am a sinner, and
you forgave me when I was not worthy of forgiveness. You sent your
own Son to die in my place. Sin is sin. All of us have sinned. The one
I need to forgive has no greater sin than mine. He is just as worthy
of your forgiveness as I am and has done no worse than I have.

Now Lord, please be near to my friend and bless him with what is
needed in his life. Draw him closer to you. Purify me from all
unforgiveness and remind me daily that he is washed in the blood
just as I am.

Continue to teach me your will about forgiveness. Thank you,
Lord God, for already answering this prayer and setting my heart in
order so I can serve you. Unforgiveness only destroys me, but your
forgiveness gives me life.

In Jesus' name I pray. Amen.

Ron

He who cannot forgive others destroys the bridge
over which he himself must pass.
                                —George Herbert

God, I Just Lost My Best Friend

I tell you the truth, whoever hears my word and believes him who sent me has eternal life and will not be condemned; he has crossed over from death to life.

—John 5:24

Oh God, today I really hurt! I feel totally empty! I miss Bill's strength, his telling me I am beautiful, and his confidence in me. He was my cheerleader, my best friend. Oh, God! He is gone!

I miss Bill's crooked smile, his twinkling eyes, his "Hi hon, I'm home." Our marriage was one that was constantly growing toward you, Father. You see, God, Bill and I truly became *one,* and I lost it all to death. We knew each other's thoughts and we sought your will for our lives.

It was your will, God, to take Bill to a far better place. I held his hand and told him to stop fighting. "It's okay to go home. I can make it, Honey." He squeezed my hand and died.

My best friend is gone! I still hurt, God! I'll never be the same again.

I can't make it without you, Lord, without your love. You have walked me through many things over the past eighteen years. You always gave me a best friend (after you). You know all my needs.

In closing, God, would you do me one more favor? Tell my Bill I still love him and that "it's still okay, Honey." (I miss you, Bill.)

In Jesus' name I pray. Amen.

Dolores

Eternity is increasingly a world that I am attracted to.
—Bob Buford

God, I Just Buried *a* Parent

Do not let your hearts be troubled. Trust in God; trust also in me. In my Father's house are many rooms; if it were not so, I would have told you. I am going there to prepare a place for you. And if I go and prepare a place for you, I will come back and take you to be with me that you also may be where I am.

—John 14:1-3

Dear God, I just saw my mother's burial, and I'm not sure how I'm going to make it without her. As my brother placed freshly cut irises on her casket, I could see that his heart was breaking as well. Lord, my father will miss her so much. It hurts me to see him weep.

I can't imagine life without her. I try to think of anyone who could fill Mother's place just a little, and the only one I can think of is you. Now, by your strength, Lord, I must go on without her.

Father, thank you for the assurance that Mom is now more alive than ever. What a comfort to know she is experiencing a dimension of life that I have not yet known! Now she enjoys your touch and your gaze. I am thankful that she gave her heart to you while she was on earth so that she was able to enter into your fullness.

Lord Jesus, thank you for preparing for my precious mom a home for an eternal dwelling place. Amen.

Mary

No one is born a Christian; the choice is up to each individual whether or not he or she will follow Christ.

God, I Need *a* Miracle

Now to him who is able to do immeasurably more than
all we ask or imagine, according to his power that is at
work within us, to him be glory! Amen.

—Ephesians 3:20-21

Heavenly Father, I know you hear me when I call, because you are my Father and you will withhold nothing from me that is good. Lord, you know I need a miracle in my life. Please increase my faith so that I can see that mountain removed. It is too big for me to deal with, but I know that nothing is too big for you.

Lord God, help me to learn your Word so that I will surely know that life and death are in the power of your tongue. Help me to choose life at moments when all else seems too big. You are the strength of my life. There is no one else whom I need.

Lord Jesus, if there is any unforgiveness in my life, show it to me. Cleanse me and make me clean. Release my heart and my mind to see you more clearly and to recognize what you have already done in my life. Let me see and accept all you have for me. Let me not be ashamed of the miracles you perform, but give me courage to proclaim them, to your glory. Amen.

Susan

Faith is a
    Fantastic
    Adventure
    In
    Trusting
    Him.

—Corrie ten Boom

PART 8

Prayers *for* Godliness *and* Obedience

71. Holy Spirit, Give Me a Greater Desire to Pray
    Philippians 4:6-7

72. Holy Spirit, Give Me a Greater Desire to Read the Bible
    1 Peter 2:2

73. Holy Spirit, Give Me a Greater Desire to Be Like Jesus
    Ephesians 5:1-2

74. Holy Spirit, Give Me a Greater Desire to Be Humble
    1 Peter 5:6

75. Holy Spirit, Give Me a Greater Desire to Forgive Others
    Luke 11:4

76. Holy Spirit, Give Me a Greater Capacity to Love the
    Unlovely
    Luke 10:33-34

77. Holy Spirit, Give Me a Greater Passion to Give to Others
    Matthew 10:42; 25:40

78. Holy Spirit, Give Me a Greater Commitment to Walk by
    Faith
    2 John 6

79. Holy Spirit, Give Me a Greater Compassion for the Lost
    Matthew 9:36

80. Holy Spirit, Give Me a Greater Courage to Share My Faith
    Acts 1:8

Holy Spirit, Give Me
a Greater Desire *to* Pray

Do not be anxious about anything, but in everything, by prayer and petition, with thanksgiving, present your requests to God. And the peace of God, which transcends all understanding, will guard your hearts and your minds in Christ Jesus.

—Philippians 4:6–7

Dear heavenly Father, sometimes it's hard for me to know where to start praying or to know what to pray for. It seems easier to go through life on my own and muddle through. Life gets so hectic that it often becomes a burden to pray. I don't want to take the time. And I'm afraid I won't get the answer I want or any answer at all.

Lord, all of these fears, doubts, and time constraints are obstacles that I cannot overcome on my own. I need your wisdom, your power, your strength, and your guidance to be able to come to you with my decisions, activities, and everything in my life.

Lord, work in my heart and give me a new desire to talk to you. Lead me to parts of Scripture that will encourage me. Help me to feel your infinite unconditional love. Fill me with a desire to come to you in prayer for every aspect of my life. Thank you for your patience with my spiritual growth and for your love.

I ask this in Jesus' name. Amen.

Julie

Expect an answer. If no answer is desired, why pray?
True prayer has in it a strong element of expectancy.

—R. M. Offord

Holy Spirit, Give Me *a* Greater Desire *to* Read *the* Bible

Like newborn babies, crave pure spiritual milk, so that by it you may grow up in your salvation.

—1 Peter 2:2

Father, I pray that you will use the Holy Spirit to help me have a greater desire to read my Bible, to help me understand what I read, and to help me retain your message from your Holy Word. Also, I pray that the Spirit will teach me to use what I read from my Bible in my daily walk with you. Then help me to reach others with the good news of Jesus Christ that is found in your Word.

I pray that you will continue to make my Bible study exciting to me and that I will grasp what my teachers are teaching me. I also want to thank you for the new Christian friends that I have found in the last seven months since I came to know you. I hope I will continue to meet new friends as I walk with you. Friends have meant very much to me.

Help me to be like a newborn baby and desire spiritual milk so that I will grow in the grace of your salvation. Continue in me the new and exciting growth I have experienced so far.

I ask this in your name. Amen.

Michelle

The one thing we need is to know God better.

—J. Hudson Taylor

Holy Spirit, Give Me *a* Greater Desire *to* Be Like Jesus

Be imitators of God, therefore, as dearly loved children and live a life of love, just as Christ loved us and gave himself up for us as a fragrant offering and sacrifice to God.

—Ephesians 5:1-2

Father, it's me again. Imitating as a child is simply to follow you, Daddy, to run after you, to want to be with you, to want to be like you, to let you control. To trust you is what I want.

Lord, I desire to be like you. I want to desire you and not waste my time on distractions. I want to be like you and sweetly reflect you.

Lord, help me to be willing to be a sacrifice, pleasing to you. Develop in me the love that you want to show to the rest of the world. To walk your way whatever the cost is difficult and scary sometimes, but I want to do what you have in mind for me.

Thank you for the promise of your presence, for the promise of your work in me, for the pleasure you take in your children who want to imitate you. Amen.

Bev

To be a Christian is to obey Christ no matter how you feel.

—Henry Ward Beecher

Holy Spirit, Give Me *a* Greater Desire *to* Be Humble

Humble yourselves, therefore, under God's mighty hand, that he may lift you up in due time.

—1 Peter 5:6

Lord, I have struggled to make two phrases part of my life. The first is John the Baptist's on the coming of Jesus' ministry: "He must become greater; I must become less" [John 3:30]. Lord, help me to recognize through your Holy Spirit the times when I must become less so that you may become greater. Let your Spirit gently remind me to let go when I desire most to hold on. Fill my heart with those desires that are consistent with your kingdom.

The second phrase, Lord, is what Jesus prayed prior to his crucifixion: "Father . . . not my will, but yours be done" [Luke 22:42]. God, I am a proud person, actually arrogant. You have changed me through your Spirit. Develop in me full maturity in Christ. Help me turn my will over to you.

Lord, fill me with your Spirit that I might humble myself in your presence. I know I can't be truly humble unless your Spirit fills me every day and the mind of Christ renews my thoughts and attitudes.

I am a new creation still under construction. I choose to worship you, my Creator, and I ask for your help, through your Spirit, in worshiping you alone. Amen.

Bill

I believe the first test of a truly great man is his humility.

—John Ruskin

Holy Spirit, Give Me *a* Greater Desire *to* Forgive Others

Forgive us our sins, for we also forgive everyone who sins against us. And lead us not into temptation.
—Luke 11:4

Dear Lord, I need to ask you to forgive me for my sins. I realize the sacrifice for my sin is your finished work on the cross. Thank you!

I often think of what I have done in falling short of your will for my life. I also become anxious and angry from what others have done to hurt me. Put in my heart the desire and ability to forgive other people's sins so that I will be released to confess my sins against you and them. I do not want to dwell on others' sins against me.

As I pray, I know I am to be transformed into a person who more and more values life as opportunity for service and prayer. Lord, impact me so strongly and deeply with your grace that it shatters my self-absorption and replaces it with genuine concern for others.

In thanksgiving for your promise of peace and for Jesus who guards my heart and mind, Amen.

Roy

They who forgive most, shall be most forgiven.
—Josiah W. Bailey

Holy Spirit, Give Me *a* Greater Capacity *to* Love *the* Unlovely

But a Samaritan, as he traveled, came where the man was; and when he saw him, he took pity on him. He went to him and bandaged his wounds, pouring on oil and wine. Then he put the man on his own donkey, took him to an inn and took care of him.

—Luke 10:33-34

Dear Father in heaven, I pray for a greater capacity to love the unlovely. Help me not to judge a person because of what he or she appears to be on the outside, but let me see the real person inside.

Lord, you have blessed me abundantly. Help me to care and be concerned about others who may not have as much as I.

Lord, give me compassion to feel what another feels. Help me to understand another person's need. I know you have made us all in your image, and I pray that I won't forget that. Allow me to be able to accept any person at whatever stage he or she is in life.

May your grace and your love be shown to me as you show me how to love the unlovely. Amen.

Jan

The purpose of life is to serve and to show compassion and the will to help others. Only then have we ourselves become true human beings.

—Albert Schweitzer

Holy Spirit, Give Me *a* Greater Passion *to* Give *to* Others

And if anyone gives even a cup of cold water to one of these little ones because he is my disciple, I tell you the truth, he will certainly not lose his reward.
—Matthew 10:42

The King will reply, "I tell you the truth, whatever you did for one of the least of these brothers of mine, you did for me."
—Matthew 25:40

Dear heavenly Father, often I'm so wrapped up in my own life that I don't see beyond myself. Between work, children, and the house, I find too many things that deter me from serving others.

Lord God, my prayer to you is for a driving passion within myself to give to others, to serve them not with a guilt-driven motive but with the love that you have given me.

You, Jesus, never gave in to those selfish desires that can overtake us, but you gave of yourself to the point of death. I ask for that same giving spirit so that others may see Christ in me.

I thank you in advance for answering this prayer, because I believe in your precious love for me. I ask all this in Jesus' name. Amen.

Sheila

It is possible to give without loving, but it is impossible to love without giving.
—R. Braunstein

Holy Spirit, Give Me *a* Greater Commitment *to* Walk *by* Faith

This is love: that we walk in obedience to his commands.
As you have heard from the beginning, his command is
that you walk in love.

—2 John 6

Father, often a restless anxiety penetrates deep within me. My heart lacks the peace and assurance that I should have when I walk side-by-side with you.

Sometimes the turmoil can be overwhelming, causing me to focus all of my energies and attention on the issue or problem at hand. I search within myself for the answers but do not always search for your solutions. I may pray earnestly to you for your help, but am I really turning it all over to you? I say that I trust you, but I don't.

When my heart and my thoughts are consumed by what I want to be, I lose the perspective of who I am in relation to who you are. I know you love me and want the very best for me, although I probably will never understand all of it in my time on earth. I must trust you to put me in the right places at the right times to fulfill your will for my life.

I pray to you now, Father, that you will cause my heart and my mind to perceive your plan for my life, particularly when things are not going as I think they should. I pray for a constant sense of peace and the assurance that you are in control. Amen.

Kirsten

It is easy to praise when things go right; it is more precious to praise when things go wrong.

Holy Spirit, Give Me *a* Greater Compassion *for the* Lost

When he saw the crowds, he had compassion on them, because they were harassed and helpless, like sheep without a shepherd.

—Matthew 9:36

Dear Father in heaven, please work in my heart to give me a greater compassion for the lost souls of this world. I thank you, Father, for the assurance of eternal life that I have through your Son, Jesus.

Father, let me never forget for a moment the inheritance I have in Christ. Instill in me a genuine desire to tell as many people as possible about your good news. Often you are the only one I can turn to. Help me to think of others who don't know you and don't have that assurance in their lives.

Father, please give me a conviction that forces action. I pray to you, Lord, to use me, according to your will, to reach out to those who are living their lives without you. In Jesus' name, Amen.

Steve

Your great employment is to bring the individual souls of men to Christ.

—E. N. Kirk

Holy Spirit, Give Me *a* Greater Courage *to* Share My Faith

But you will receive power when the Holy Spirit comes
on you; and you will be my witnesses in Jerusalem, and
in all Judea and Samaria, and to the ends of the earth.
—Acts 1:8

Lord Jesus, I love you. Thank you for dying on the cross for me and rising victorious so that I can live a new life. You are precious.

Holy Spirit, you have come into my life not only to comfort me but also to give me power from on high. Thank you for your help. Now I want to ask for greater wisdom in knowing what to say to people who ask me about my faith in Christ. Please make me sensitive to others when I tell them about my faith.

Lord, you have given us power to do your work. Open me up to your guidance and give me the courage to go where you want me to go and to proclaim your Word.

I know that I will not be alone. Holy Spirit, you are abiding in me and go with me. Even though I may feel alone in this world I actually am not, because you are in me. Let me never forget that no matter where I am, there you are. I can do little in my own strength.

Thank you, Holy Spirit, for the power, strength, comfort, courage, and wisdom you will give me to share with others.

In Jesus' name I pray. Amen.

Susan

I reckon him a Christian indeed who is not ashamed of the Gospel, nor a shame to it.
—Matthew Henry

PART 9

Prayers *for* Other People *in* My Life

A Prayer *for a* Friend Who Is Far *from* God

My brothers, if one of you should wander from the truth and someone should bring him back, remember this: Whoever turns a sinner from the error of his way will save him from death and cover over a multitude of sins.

—James 5:19-20

Precious Lord, my dearly beloved friend is far away from you. How can I bring her back? She strives hard, she longs deeply as she seeks the truth—*her* truth, perhaps—but it's you she longs for.

She is overwhelmed by all the values of the world. She is good and decent by worldly standards—a great contribution to this earth and its grim society. She does what appears to be right.

She says she believes that you really exist and maybe Christ really did die on the cross, but then, maybe not. That's it. Oh, I feel so terribly frustrated!

Help me be her friend. Help me to cherish our friendship. Lord, should I say more to her, or should I be your witness by merely setting a silent example? Sometimes that seems hard. What if I really show that I, too, am human and have faults and sin?

In my weaknesses and my strengths let me be your light that draws your children back to you. And Lord, please remember my friend. Amen.

Sharon

As you draw near to the poor, the Savior will come nearer to you.

—George C. Lorimer

A Prayer *for a* Dysfunctional Friend

We who are strong ought to bear with the failings of the
weak and not to please ourselves. Each of us should please
his neighbor for his good, to build him up.

—Romans 15:1-2

Heavenly Father, I don't know how to pray for my friend. His life is a mess. He is unhappy and confused, moving in all the wrong directions. He seems to make the same wrong choices again and again. Some of his relationships appear to be harmful instead of helpful. The people he trusts drag him down. I think he tries, but he doesn't seem able to find his way out of the maze.

I know our backgrounds and our choices bring certain consequences. But Lord, thank you for setting us free from the endless repetition of our mistakes and situations. Maybe my friend doesn't know your powerful love can free him from this kind of bondage.

I pray you will arrange the circumstances of his life so that he will find an open door to your love and your guidance. Help him walk through that opening, reach out, and take your hand. Give him the opportunity to really hear your Word and to understand. Lord, protect him as he searches.

Lord Jesus, guide me so that as his friend I will know how to be sensitive and truly helpful. Help me be strong and lead him to your love. Amen.

Patricia

We have, all of us, sufficient fortitude to bear the misfortunes of others.

—La Rochefoucauld

A Prayer *for a* Sick Friend

Is any one of you sick? He should call the elders of the
church to pray over him and anoint him with oil in the
name of the Lord. And the prayer offered in faith will
make the sick person well; the Lord will raise him up. If
he has sinned, he will be forgiven.

—James 5:14–15

Dear Father in heaven, we recognize that we have our limits. Physically we are susceptible to the flu or cancer, to allergies or heart attacks; emotionally we are sometimes at the top and other times discouraged, brokenhearted, or in despair; spiritually we may drift far from our walk with you.

Yet we are reminded by your Word that while we are weak you are always strong, and that even in the midst of our weakness you can still accomplish your work.

Thank you, Lord, for the comfort of your presence during these times and for the loving support and encouragement you give us through our brothers and sisters in Christ.

Father, I turn over to you the weakness of my friend. I do not know yet what you will do or accomplish, but I pray for your will to be done. I pray that our friendship will grow. O Lord, as you and I and my friend face this time, help us to walk through it together. Amen.

Mike

Difficulties provide a platform on which the Lord can display His power.

—J. Hudson Taylor

A Prayer *for a* Dying Friend

Even though I walk through the valley of the shadow of death, I will fear no evil, for you are with me; your rod and your staff, they comfort me.

—Psalm 23:4

Dearest heavenly Father, how can it be that my dearest friend is dying and I am weak in my ability to be strong for her? When I talk with her, my heart is so full of pain the tears will not stop flowing. I want her to remain here on earth, even though I know that when you take her from me she will be at peace with you and her pain and suffering will be over.

Thank you, Father, that you have been her Shepherd, that you have led her safely through dark and difficult days. Please give her strength as she prepares to leave loved ones behind.

Help me to be stronger for her, to remember that she has chosen salvation, and that her life will continue in a more beautiful position than she now is in. Lord, it is difficult for me to lose those I care about.

Thank you, Father, for loving her in an unselfish way. Forgive me for being selfish, and help me to be more like you.

I pray this in the precious name of Jesus. Amen.

Anne

The truest end of life is to know the life that never ends.

—Beresford

A Prayer *for a* Friend Making Wrong Choices

Brothers, if someone is caught in a sin, you who are spiritual should restore him gently. But watch yourself, or you also may be tempted.

—Galatians 6:1

Dear heavenly Father, I am thankful for this opportunity to come before you with a special need. Father, I have a friend who is making some wrong choices for her life. I have tried talking to her in subtle ways, in direct ways, and even wrote her a long letter expressing my opinion of the situation.

I recognize that I do not have any control over the choices that this friend is making for her life, and I am in no position to judge her. But I feel that these choices are going to end up being very damaging to her emotionally and physically. She is a very strong-willed woman. She also is a very sad and lonely woman.

Father, I pray that you will supply me with the guidance and the wisdom to be a true friend. Help me to recognize that you are working in her life through these situations.

I pray that if it is your will you will use me in the life of my friend. Help me to see the larger picture and to rest in your will. Help me to be patient and kind when we spend time together. Thank you for your wisdom, guidance, and never-ending love.

I pray these things in Jesus' name. Amen.

Jennifer

God loves us the way we are, but he loves us too much to leave us that way.

—Leighton Ford

A Prayer *for a* Friend *in* Trouble

For in the day of trouble he will keep me safe in his
dwelling; he will hide me in the shelter of his tabernacle
and set me high upon a rock.

—Psalm 27:5

Most gracious heavenly Father, thank you for all of the beautiful and wonderful things that you have put into my life, especially my friends.

One of these friends brings me to you today. You know that my friend is in trouble and hurting right now.

Let this friend be reassured that you are always with her, no matter how bad things are or seem to be. Let your peace surround her, and let the knowledge of your presence be a source of strength for her now.

Let my friend be reminded that you are sovereign over all things. I pray that all things will work in her life according to your will.

I pray that my friend will ask you for renewed strength and guidance and, most especially, will trust in you. Give her strength to get through each day.

Strengthen me as her friend to help her in any way that I can, to see the ways in which I can be of help. Show me how to love and care for her.

All of these things I ask in your Son's holy name. Amen.

Kay

If I can stop one heart from breaking, I shall not live in vain.

—Emily Dickinson

A Prayer *for a* Friend
Doubting That God Is Able

*Therefore he is able to save completely those who come
to God through him, because he always lives to intercede
for them.*

—Hebrews 7:25

Lord, I want to thank you that you are a friend who sticks closer
than a brother. Regardless of any situation your children face, you
are in that situation leading, guiding, and loving.

My friend is having a difficult time believing in your ability to
meet a present need. First, I ask you to give him assurance of your
love and your continued presence in his life. Help him to see your
greatness and majesty. I know that when he sees you his problem
will look very small to him.

Next, give him faith in your ability and power to meet this need.
Help him see that nothing is impossible with you and that you are a
mountain-moving God.

Finally, help me to stand by him, encourage him, and minister
your love and grace during this time.

I believe you are able to do anything, God. Amen.

Kathy

Are you dismayed, lonely, afraid,
　　thinking yourself forsaken?
God is your stay,
Trust him and pray;
　　new hope he will awaken!
—Selma Lagerstrom
(Tr. E. Gustav Johnson)

A Prayer *for a* Friend
Facing *a* Crisis

But encourage one another daily, as long as it is called Today, so that none of you may be hardened by sin's deceitfulness.

—Hebrews 3:13

Heavenly Father, it's about my new friend. He's in a bunch of legal trouble. He faces problems on all sides. He's destroying good relationships and hurting himself by his lifestyle. Lord, I don't know what to do.

My friend needs a miracle in his life. Actually he needs a lot of miracles. You are the only one I know who is in the habit of granting miracles.

God, I remember how you helped Max in his crises. He was angry at the world. He was even so angry at you that he denied your existence. But you answered prayer and changed him. Now he serves you in Tunisia.

God, I remember how you helped Jeff in his crisis. His family was devastated, and he lacked anything stable in his life. Yet, he and his family came to you. Praise you!

Now, God, about my friend: I pray that you will interrupt and invade his life. May your Holy Spirit bring about conviction so that he will repent and become your son.

God, I ask in the name of the one who chose to die for my friend: Jesus. Amen.

Bill

Stand strong in God . . . for after winter, summer comes; after night, the day returns; and after a storm, calm is restored.

—Thomas à Kempis

A Prayer *for a* Friend *with* Unspoken Needs

And pray in the Spirit on all occasions with all kinds of prayers and requests. With this in mind, be alert and always keep on praying for all the saints.

—Ephesians 6:18

Lord, I thank you that you know all things. You know when I sit down and when I get up. You understand my every thought. You examine every step I take. You are intimately acquainted with everything I do. Even before there is a word on my tongue—it is amazing to me—you know what I will say. Though I do not know the particulars of my friend's unspoken prayer request, I know you do.

I thank you that your Spirit also helps me when I am weak, especially when I do not know how to pray as I should. Thank you for your prayers for me and for my friend. I find comfort in your knowledge of my friend's needs. Thank you for not missing a thing.

Lord, help him to keep his eyes on you. I thank you and praise you that, as I bring him to you, I can leave him in your hands knowing you will do what is best for him from your heavenly and perfect perspective.

I praise you for being the perfect friend. Amen.

Michael

He prays well who is so absorbed with God that he does not know he is praying.

—St. Francis de Sales

A Prayer *for a* Friend Who Needs Salvation

*That if you confess with your mouth, "Jesus is Lord,"
and believe in your heart that God raised him from the
dead, you will be saved. . . . For, "Everyone who calls on
the name of the Lord will be saved."*

—Romans 10:9, 13

Dear God, you know that I want my friend to accept you as Lord and Savior, but it seems he will never respond to you. I know you have come so that all people might choose to know you, and I ask you to help me to keep trusting in your Word. I want to leave him in your hands because I know you are the one who will draw him to you. I also ask your help to live my life so he can see that you really make a difference in people's lives.

Please give me the words to say and remind me when to stop talking and to listen.

Help him to understand that he is a sinner and to see that your Son's death on the cross is the only way that he can receive forgiveness for his sins. Help him to understand your love in such a way that he wants you in his life. I beg for your leading in my life so that I can show your love to him.

I am terrified to think my friend could spend eternity without you. I pray that he will respond to your gift of salvation before it is too late.

Thank you for hearing my prayer. I am grateful that you are a God of hope. Amen.

Brent

How else but through a broken heart may Lord Christ enter in?

—Oscar Wilde

PART 10

Prayers *for* Single Parents

Father in Heaven,
My Children Need You

Then little children were brought to Jesus for him to place his hands on them and pray for them. But the disciples rebuked those who brought them. Jesus said, "Let the little children come to me, and do not hinder them, for the kingdom of heaven belongs to such as these."
—Matthew 19:13-14

Father in heaven, my children do not know they need you. I know you, and I know that in your Word you have said that no one should hinder the children. We all should come to you as small children, with openness and trust and total dependence on you. Second Peter 3:9 says you are not slow to keep your promise and you are patient, not wanting anyone to perish. I trust in you, Father, and I claim this promise for my children.

I pray that you will open their eyes and turn them from darkness to light, from the influence of Satan to you. Help them to see their need for forgiveness of their sins. Encourage them, somehow, to step by faith in Christ.

Father, I promise I will continue to keep praying for my dear children, and I ask you to fill them with the knowledge of your will through every event and circumstance in their lives—even the bad ones.

I thank you, Lord, for your promise, and I hold on to it with hope. Amen.

Betty

Train up a child in the way he should go and walk there yourself once in a while.
—Josh Billings

92

Father *in* Heaven, I Can't Keep Up This Pace Much Longer

Then Jesus told his disciples a parable to show them that they should always pray and not give up.

—Luke 18:1

Dear Father in heaven, the day has once again turned into night. Thank you for holding me up and giving me strength to cope with the pressures and demands from the pace I keep.

Just as I'm ready to say I can't do this another day, you tap me on the shoulder and remind me you will never give me more than I can bear. You know my limits, and I thank you for reminding me that I will make it through each tomorrow that comes.

Each day I see a new way to slow the pace or at least to make it easier to handle. I am grateful for reminders of you as each day ends.

Please help me let go of the day, to clear my mind, and to prepare my body for a restful night. You are my strength when I am awake and my peace when I sleep. In Jesus' name, Amen.

Colleen

Sometimes God calms the storm, and sometimes He lets the storm rage and calms His child.

—Donna Wallis

Father *in* Heaven, I Need Some Personal Time

The LORD *Almighty is with us; the God of Jacob is our fortress. Come and see the works of the* LORD, *the desolations he has brought on the earth. He makes wars cease to the ends of the earth; he breaks the bow and shatters the spear, he burns the shields with fire. Be still, and know that I am God; I will be exalted among the nations, I will be exalted in the earth.*

—Psalm 46:7–10

Single Parent's Prayer

Lord, grant me time enough to do all the chores, join in the games, help with the lessons, say the night prayers, and still have a few moments left for me.

Lord, grant me energy enough to be bread baker and breadwinner, knee patcher and peacemaker, ball player and bill juggler.

Lord, grant me hands to wipe away the tears, to reach out when I'm needed, to hug and to hold, to tickle and to touch.

Lord, grant me heart enough to share and to care, to listen and to understand, and to make a loving home for my family.

Author unknown

Spend plenty of time with God; let other things go, but don't neglect him.

—Oswald Chambers

Father *in* Heaven, I Need Friends

*But if we walk in the light, as he is in the light, we have
fellowship with one another, and the blood of Jesus, his
Son, purifies us from all sin.*

—1 John 1:7

Father, I want to thank you for being my best friend. You've never
let me down and you always pick me up when others let me down
(whether they do it intentionally or unintentionally). You've led me
to some very close friends who make me accountable to you and
encourage me when I am sad. They help me seek your advice on the
small as well as the large decisions that I need to make in my everyday life. They accept me for who I am so I do not need to be a
people pleaser or put on any masks.

You have created me with a need to share my innermost thoughts
with friends. It took me many years to discover that I could not pick
all my friends myself, but that you had the right ones in mind for
me. Now that I have asked you to show them to me, I'm finding
many. Thank you for teaching me that I can have friends of different
ages and backgrounds. Help me to open the gifts you have given me
in friends of all kinds. Amen.

Karilyn

Blessed are they that have the gift of making friends,
for it is one of God's best gifts. It involves many
things, but above all, the power of going out of one's
self, and appreciating whatever is noble and loving
in another.

—Thomas Hughes

Father *in* Heaven, My Children Are Drifting Away

Train a child in the way he should go, and when he is old he will not turn from it.

—Proverbs 22:6

Do not let any unwholesome talk come out of your mouths, but only what is helpful for building others up according to their needs, that it may benefit those who listen.

—Ephesians 4:29

Lord, this is not what I thought your plan would be for my life. I never would have pictured myself as a divorced woman. Lord, you saw how happy our family was before its breakup, how sweet and well-adjusted our children were. You know how I've prayed for these children each day. How will they grow up to love and serve you now? All of their values are shaken by what has happened.

What can I do to help reestablish their values? They seem to have forgotten all they were ever taught. How can I counteract what they are seeing and hearing from their father? What is left for me now? How can this be part of your good plan for me?

Thank you for Romans 4:18–21 from your Word today. Help me to have faith as Abraham did when seemingly there was no hope. You have promised never to leave or forsake me.

I will trust you because you are sovereign. Amen.

Becky

Prayer is the mortar that holds our house together.
—Mother Teresa

Father *in* Heaven, My Job Is Not Working Out

The Lord will guide you always; he will satisfy your needs in a sun-scorched land and will strengthen your frame. You will be like a well-watered garden, like a spring whose waters never fail.

—Isaiah 58:11

Dear Father in heaven, my job is not working out. It is beginning to be a real chore to get out of bed and go to work every morning. My boss is really hard to deal with. Her temper causes her to fly off the handle frequently.

My job is boring and is not what I really want to be doing. It is taking me too long to get through school so I can get a better job.

Lord, it is hard to work where other people are quick to point out my mistakes but totally ignore their own mistakes. I know you understand what I am going through. I am tired of feeling unappreciated. I am tired of everyone making demands on me.

Lord, teach me understanding in dealing with my boss and coworkers. Teach me patience in learning to wait on you for guidance on my job and schooling. I know you have something better in store for me.

I will draw from your fruit of patience. Amen.

Linda

Never think that God's delays are God's denials. Hold on; hold fast; hold out. Patience is genius.

—Comte de Buffon

Father *in* Heaven, I Can't Pay *the* Bills This Month

Give us each day our daily bread.
—Luke 11:3

Heavenly Father, it's me again. Thank you for your love and your care. You always provide what I need, and it seems I'm always in need.

Lord, I am not sure how I'll pay all my bills this month. I know you already have a plan; I'm just not sure what it is. You know how discouraged I can get.

I work and budget and try to conserve, but it always seems the black on white paper must be written in invisible ink. The money seems to disappear from right out of my hands. Help me to see, to understand even another or better way that I don't know now.

When I do get frustrated, Lord, help me to remember: I'm not hungry, I'm not cold, I'm not homeless, and I'm not unloved! Above all else, help me remember I am yours and that you do love me more than anyone else ever has or will.

In Jesus' name, Amen.

Brenda

He has the film of my whole life in view, and not just the snapshot of my present situation.
—W. Trobisch

Father *in* Heaven, We Need *a* Place *to* Live

*And my God will meet all your needs according to his
glorious riches in Christ Jesus.*

—Philippians 4:19

Okay, Lord, I admit, I did make some bad choices. I am tired of
hearing everyone tell me that I have made my bed and now I have to
sleep in it. But now I do not know where that bed is going to be in
about thirty days. And my kids do not even have beds.

Lord, what am I going to do? I have tried every resource and
agency under the sun. Does anyone really care, especially about someone who has made a mess of her life as I have done? I want to
believe that you care, and I promise to trust you.

Give me courage to face the people at my church and my parents.
Help me to be honest and courageous to do what I need to do to
improve this deplorable situation I am in—again.

Father, help me believe that you will supply all my needs. Help
me to know your resources for my life and my children. Help me to
believe that these resources are really for us.

I love you, Lord. I want to obey you and be responsible. I want to
trust you. Thank you for understanding and loving me.

Thanks for all that you have and will provide. Amen.

Darlene

All the lessons he shall send are the sweetest;
and his training, in the end, is completest.

—F. R. Havergal

Father *in* Heaven, My Former Spouse Has Done It Again

I have set the LORD always before me. Because he is at my right hand, I will not be shaken.

—Psalm 16:8

Dear Father in heaven, I'm so mad right now. I know I'm supposed to love my enemy, but this doesn't even make sense. Did you see what he did again? Lord, it would be so much easier to love him if you would zap him—just a little. Please do something.

Okay, okay, I'll be calm. Let's talk. I'm angry and terribly hurt. I don't want to feel this way. It makes me want to lash back, but I know if I do, it will only keep a vicious cycle of bitterness going and growing. That is not your will for my life. I know whose will it is.

Father, please help me walk the path you want for me. Give me your love for him; I have none of my own. I know he is reacting from his pain; I don't want to do the same. Through your strength and grace I can be a blessing.

Please fill me with your Holy Spirit. Help me take comfort in you and keep my tongue in check. Lord, keep me from antagonizing him. Cover me with your love right now, because I really need it. Amen.

Jean

If you find yourself growing angry at someone, pray for him; anger cannot live in an atmosphere of prayer.

—W. T. McElroy

Father *in* Heaven, Are You Still There?

*As I was with Moses, so I will be with you; I will never
leave you nor forsake you.*

—Joshua 1:5

*Then you will call, and the LORD will answer; you will
cry for help, and he will say: Here am I. ". . . Do away
with the yoke of oppression, with the pointing finger and
malicious talk."*

—Isaiah 58:9

Dear Father, are you still there? It's been a constant struggle this
week. Work is hectic and relationships are strained at times. Then
there is the past. It rears its ugly head at the least opportune times.
Sometimes when all this happens I lose the sense of your presence,
of your being by my side, and the peace that you bring.

You have said in the Bible over and over, "I will never leave you
nor forsake you." As I pause now, the truth of that hits home inside.
You, God, care for all your children and you are not going to run
from me. During those hectic times in life, you are at my side. My
greatest need is to learn to slow down and savor your presence and
help, to realize that you are always with me. That encouragement
fills my soul.

Father, during the busy and hectic times of life bring the realiza-
tion to me that you are with me and nothing can ever drive you
away. Amen.

Richard

Thou hast made us for thyself, and the heart never
resteth till it findeth rest in thee.

—St. Augustine

Final Prayer

Here I am! I stand at the door and knock. If anyone hears my voice and opens the door, I will come in and eat with him, and he with me.

—Revelation 3:20

Father in heaven, I come to you just the way I am. As I pray the prayer I realize that it really is not a final prayer, but it is a prayer for a brand-new beginning.

I confess that my life has been separated from you. I have not lived according to your purpose or plan for my life. I have been selfish. I have loved myself and everything around me, but not you. Please forgive me of my sins.

Thank you for sending your only Son, Jesus, to die on the cross to remove the guilt and burden of my sin. Thank you for your love for me. I am overwhelmed by your desire for me to be your child.

Therefore, I yield my life to Christ. Jesus, please take control. Fill me with your mind and your Spirit. My desire is for you to be the master of my life.

Based on the promise above, I thank you for entering the door of my life and becoming my Lord and Savior. Thank you for residing in my life and giving me a new start—a brand new life.

Give me the courage to live for you every day. In the name of Jesus I pray. Amen.

_____

(Your Name)

Salvation is free for you because someone else paid.